TUTANKHAMUN

TUTANKHAMUN
THE TREASURES OF THE GOLDEN KING

Kate Santon

Bath · New York · Singapore · Hong Kong · Cologne · Delhi · Melbourne

This is a Parragon Book
First published in 2007

Parragon Books Ltd
Queen Street House
4 Queen Street
Bath, BA1 1HE

Produced by Atlantic Publishing

See page 96 for
photograph copyright details
Text © Parragon Books Ltd 2007

A CIP catalogue record for this book is
available from the British Library.

ISBN 978-1-4054-8811-2
Printed in China

Contents

Introduction 7

Discoveries 8

The World of Tutankhamun 30

Exploring Tutankhamun's Tomb 50

Introduction

Tutankhamun lived during one of the most extraordinary periods in the history of Ancient Egypt, a time of enormous upheaval but also one of enormous wealth and influence, and of great artistic achievement. He was, however, a very minor part of all this despite being the ruler; he came to the throne as a child and died before he was 20. During his reign Egypt returned to the old religion, turning away from the 'heresy' of Akhenaten. Very few people, other than specialists and scholars, knew his name. All this changed in 1922, when the British archaeologist Howard Carter peered through a hole he had made in a blocked doorway at the end of a passage beneath the Valley of the Kings. Glittering in the light of his candle were some of the most extraordinary archaeological treasures the world has ever seen. And what he saw was only a small part of the whole.

Luck had played a part in ensuring that the tomb survived almost intact. Tutankhamun had died unexpectedly early and been buried in an improvised tomb rather than the imposing – and more obvious – one that was being prepared. Two robberies had been detected, and the tomb resealed. Then another tomb was built close by and workmen's huts covered the entrance. It was also lucky that the tomb was found by Howard Carter. At the time archaeology, especially in Egypt, could be rather ramshackle and buccaneering, but Carter was an archaeologist of a different type. He was meticulous and careful, realised the immense significance of every single thing from the tomb, and treated it with care. From the beginning other experts were involved – something which was rare at the time but which is now commonplace – and much was saved which would otherwise have been lost. His relationships with other people and with the Egyptian government could be difficult, but through it all he kept working, not rushing at things and being as systematic as he could. He devoted 15 years to the tomb, though he died before he could complete a major publication; his three-volume book *The Tomb of Tut.ankh.amun* was designed to be a brief summary. The notes he kept still survive, and help researchers to this day.

The king's golden mask, his throne and other spectacular finds are just the beginning. For the first time it was possible to see how a king of one of the wealthiest periods in Egypt's history had been buried, and it was also possible to reconstruct what had happened in the tomb after the burial – two robberies, and two attempts at restoring an approximation of order after their discovery. Every single item from the king's tomb is of huge importance, throwing a light onto the world of the New Kingdom. They are all unique, many are great works of art in their own right, and many display extremely high levels of skill and technical sophistication.

All the finds from Tutankhamun's tomb seem as fresh and relevant today as they were on that March day over 3000 years ago when they were sealed inside the cramped subterranean chambers. Somehow they, and the young king for whom they were created, span the many centuries which have passed since then. They draw visitors in their thousands to the Egyptian Museum in Cairo, and many go on to visit his tomb where he still rests.

In Ancient Egypt, keeping someone's name alive after their death enabled them to achieve and maintain immortality. No name from the distant past is as well known as that of Tutankhamun, the young king.

Discoveries

From the earliest times, the remarkable civilisation that once flourished along the Nile has fascinated explorers and, more recently, archaeologists. The 19th and early 20th centuries saw many discoveries, culminating in the astonishing tomb of Tutankhamun.

Finding Ancient Egypt

The most obvious monuments of Egypt's past civilization have been recognised and described by travellers for thousands of years. The Pyramids excited wonder and speculation, classical writers like Herodotus gave accounts of the history and culture of this so clearly ancient land. But academic study only really began at the end of the 18th century, with Napoleon's ill-thought-out expedition to Egypt in 1798. A number of scholars travelled with his army in the hope of reporting on an anticipated triumph. That never came, but many of them became fascinated with the land they found themselves in. The most influential of these was Baron Vivant Denon who did many paintings and drawings, and went on to publish a popular and influential book when he returned to Europe. In many ways he was responsible for opening European eyes to the history of Egypt. Twenty years later Jean-François Champollion completed the decipherment of Egyptian hieroglyphics and Egyptology, the serious study of Ancient Egypt, was born.

Unfortunately this was an age of unprincipled 'collecting' and what has been referred to as the 'rape of Egypt' began: it has also been likened to looting or an archaeological gold rush. Priceless archaeological remains could be retrieved very easily, and there was a ready market – and no scruples. Nor was there any real understanding of the importance of context, of the immense and irreplaceable significance of an object or site in its complete setting. Without that, so much information is lost forever. As a result of this many museums in Europe and America have large Egyptian collections. This situation slowly began to improve, and the Egyptians also began to assert their authority over their heritage, and by the time Howard Carter made his historic discovery of the tomb of Tutankhamun the situation was somewhat different. Archaeology, and political awareness, has also changed since Carter's time and continues to do so.

The River Nile has always been of central importance to the land of Egypt; without it, and its regular floods, both life and civilization would have been impossible. In Ancient Egypt the fertile land of the Nile Valley was reserved for the living; the dead belonged in the desert west of the river, in the direction which was associated with the Afterlife. There were several centres of occupation, cities and sites which exerted a major influence. The main ones were Memphis in Lower Egypt, the north of the country, which the Ancient Egyptians knew as Inebhedj, and Thebes, much further south in Upper Egypt. Its Egyptian name was Waset. Thebes really flowered in the New Kingdom, when royal tombs were built in the Valley of the Kings. The pharaoh would move around the whole country and not simply reside in one place to the exclusion of all others other than in exceptional circumstances.

Years of study, excavation and research have produced a greater understanding of the history of Ancient Egypt, but there are still some areas of uncertainty and one of them concerns definite dates, which are still the subject of some debate. Ancient Egyptian history is broadly divided into three main 'Kingdoms', the Old, Middle and New Kingdoms. The New Kingdom, when Tutankhamun lived and died, ran from c.1550 BC to c.1070 BC. Between these three Kingdoms are shorter phases, known as the Intermediate Periods, and following the last of these comes the Late Period. There is a finer division, too: the Dynasties. Egyptian rulers were divided into 30 groups by the third century BC Egyptian historian Manetho, and these groups, marked by changes in the royal house, are still useful today. The Pyramids at Giza, for example, were constructed by three Old Kingdom pharaohs of the 4th Dynasty, Khufu, Khafre and Menkaure, long before Tutankhamun reigned; he belonged to the 18th Dynasty, a time of extraordinary wealth and power for Egypt.

Opposite: The Great Pyramids of Giza dating from third millenium BC were already ancient monuments at the time of Tutankhamun. Although Tutankhamun's treasures came to light less than 100 years ago, they have made him as famous as these ancient wonders.

Below: The ruins of the Temple of Kom Ombo, located on the Nile north of Aswan, stand at the other end of the timescale of Ancient Egypt, dating from the Ptolemaic period in second century BC. An unusual double temple, one side is dedicated to crocodile god Sobek and the other to falcon god Haroeris, also known as Horus the Elder.

Exploring the Valley of the Kings

On the far side of the Nile from Thebes, now the city of Luxor, the mountains marking the start of the desert rise above the plain in huge cliffs. The river valley plain was an ideal place for building royal mortuary temples, and in the mountains behind the cliffs were a series of dried-up water courses and ravines which could also be useful. Above these looms a pyramid-shaped mountain, called el-Qurn. It was sacred to the goddess Hathor, the Lady of the West, and beneath it lies the Valley of the Kings, the burial place of New Kingdom pharaohs.

Religious symbolism was extremely important in Ancient Egypt, and the valley was undoubtedly given a particular importance by its setting but it was also a good choice for wealthy burials for more practical reasons. It could be easily guarded – the access routes were relatively restricted – and it was comparatively remote, about 5 km away from the Nile. The major occupied areas of the west bank were several hours' walk away, going by the most accessible route. There were, however, ways through the mountains that were less easy to supervise, including one that led into it from the artisans' village of Deir el-Medina.

The valley has two separate branches, the eastern one in which most of the royal tombs have been found and a western branch which, though larger, contains fewer burials. The walls of the Valley, particularly the West Valley, have lots of smaller ravines and clefts, ideal for further obscuring tomb entrances. During the 18th Dynasty, Tutankhamun's time, members of the royal family as well as kings might also be buried there; in the next Dynasty a new valley, the Valley of the Queens, was brought into use. The last burial in the Valley took place before 1000 BC; it was abandoned, as was the village of Deir el-Medina.

Early discoveries in the Valley

Greeks were some of the earliest visitors, exploring Egypt after the conquest of Alexander. Some of the more intrepid ventured into open tombs and left carved graffiti behind them; so, later, did Roman visitors. The real explosion in activity came much later, in the nineteenth century. Baron Vivant Denon, who was in Egypt as part of Napoleon's 1798 expedition, visited the Valley and described six tombs. He returned to Europe, but other French scholars went on to produce the first map, which noted the existence of 16 tombs and marked the western branch.

The French and British representatives then started what, at times, seems like a competition to discover the most. The British Consul, Henry Salt, had an extraordinary individual on his side – Giovanni Battista Belzoni, an engineer who had previously been a strongman. Belzoni set about exploring the Valley of the Kings and made his first find in 1816; this was

the tomb of the pharaoh Ay, Tutankhamun's successor. Then began a series of explorations, often by wealthy scholars. One of these, John Gardner Wilkinson, introduced a system of numbering tombs – KV for Kings' Valley or W for West Valley, followed by a number – which is still in use today; Tutankhamun's tomb is KV62.

By the end of the nineteenth century everything became more professional, and the Egyptian Antiquities Service was formed. In 1899 the Frenchman Gaston Maspero was returned as its director after a break of 13 years, and he made a significant appointment for the archaeology of the Valley: his protégé Howard Carter became the first Chief Inspector of Antiquities for Upper Egypt. Carter laid great stress on conservation as well as on continuing exploration, and introduced electric lighting

into some of the tombs. He also approached a wealthy American, Theodore Davis, for sponsorship.

Theodore Davis

Theodore Davis is one of the key figures in the more recent history of the royal valley. An elderly financier and lawyer, he regularly travelled in Egypt but came late to Egyptology. Though enthusiastic about his new passion he was also amateurish,

Below: The pyramidal mountain of el-Qurn presides over the Valley of the Kings on the west bank of the Nile. The symbolism would have been one of the factors leading to the selection of the area as a suitable site for royal burials, and the peak was venerated.

inaccurate, had an apparent aversion to publishing his discoveries and could even be deliberately destructive. His interest in conserving and recording his finds was almost non-existent. Fortunately, he did not do much digging himself but sponsored others; unfortunately he was difficult and interfering, and there was a fairly rapid turnover in archaeologists who could work with him. These men did, however, make some remarkable discoveries. Three are particularly relevant to the story of Tutankhamun.

The tomb of Yuya and Thuya

James Quibell, who had succeeded Carter as Inspector, was excavating for Davis in 1905 when he found a little-disturbed tomb, now known as KV46. Though it was richly equipped it was not a royal burial; the occupants were a couple named Yuya and Thuya who had been the parents of Tiye, Amenhotep III's queen and (probably) Tutankhamun's grandmother. It was a small tomb but was packed with objects from floor to ceiling, and became the most remarkable Egyptian discovery ever made until the finding of Tutankhamun's burial 17 years later. Like his, it had also been disturbed and resealed.

Yuya had been the Commander of the King's Chariots, and also used the honorific title of 'God's Father', while his wife Thuya held a series of positions at court. Judging by the number of times it is repeated in her tomb her favourite title was 'Royal Mother of the Chief Wife of the King'. Both their mummies

were beautifully preserved, but they had been partly unwrapped by thieves searching for valuables. The robbers had also taken the most portable objects, though they had left many items of great beauty including a chariot and an exquisite chair known as the Chair of Sitamun, who is shown on the back panel. Sitamun was the couple's royal granddaughter, a child of their daughter Tiye and Amenhotep III, and the chair may have been an offering she made to the burial of one of her grandparents – there is some evidence that they died at different times.

The mystery of KV55

Another of Davis's excavators, Edward Ayrton, found a very different burial in 1907. It was a mess, with a jumble of fragments – including part of a shrine made for Queen Tiye – and a coffin containing a mummy. The names on the coffin had been deliberately cut out and the face had been ripped off below the level of the forehead. Despite this, more has been written about this tomb than almost any other, and that is because there is a possibility that the body in the coffin is that of the heretical ruler (and likely father of Tutankhamun), Akhenaten. But it might not be. Apart from the fact that the body is male and, from the physical evidence, a close blood relative of Tutankhamun, nothing is certain. It used to be thought that it might be the body of a shadowy individual called Smenkhkare, who may have ruled with Akhenaten for the last few years of his reign and possibly independently for two years after his death. Smenkhkare could have been a child of Akhenaten and a minor wife, as Tutankhamun appears to have been, or he could have been a younger brother; some scholars believe that Smenkhkare wasn't a he at all, but Akhenaten's queen Nefertiti under another name. This body is definitely male, however, and everything hinges on its age. Yet again the evidence is inconclusive and contradictory. Some estimates suggest that the individual was between 20 and 25: too young to be Akhenaten, though he remains the favourite candidate until the age can be determined conclusively.

Pit 54

Another 1907 discovery was even less impressive than KV55. It was a deep pit containing some large storage jars containing miscellaneous debris. Seal impressions bore the name of Tutankhamun, fragments of linen had dockets noting specific

years of his reign, and there were faded floral collars and even a miniature mask. Davis, cavalier as ever, shredded the collars to demonstrate how strong – or not – they remained after 3000 years. Originally it was thought that this material had been buried immediately after Tutankhamun's funeral; now it is known that the jars had originally been in the empty entrance corridor of his tomb. They had been placed in a pit by the authorities of the royal necropolis following the first robbery shortly after his burial, when the corridor was filled with rubble to deter future thieves.

Davis leaves the Valley

In 1909 one more small Tutankhamun-related find was made and Davis decided that this was it: he had found all that remained of Tutankhamun's missing burial. Davis announced 'I fear that the Valley of the Tombs is now exhausted', and gave up his concession to dig in it. Theodore Davis and his different archaeologists had actually missed the entrance to Tutankhamun's tomb by a distance of approximately two metres. Given his attitude to excavation, recording and the preservation of anything he found, this was probably just as well.

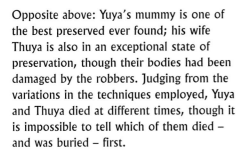

Opposite above: Yuya's mummy is one of the best preserved ever found; his wife Thuya is also in an exceptional state of preservation, though their bodies had been damaged by the robbers. Judging from the variations in the techniques employed, Yuya and Thuya died at different times, though it is impossible to tell which of them died – and was buried – first.

Opposite below: The 'Chair of Sitamun' from the tomb of the Princess Sitamun's grandparents, Yuya and Thuya. It is large enough for an adult and is in excellent condition, even the seat which is made from woven plant fibre. The back of the chair shows Sitamun; the rest of the decoration concentrates on deities who would have been particularly relevant to women, like the childbirth god Bes.

Right: Thuya's jewel box had been opened and emptied by the thieves who removed all the portable valuables from the tomb. The bottom was found under a bed, while the top lay to one side, near her wig and an alabaster vase.

Mummification

People, thought the Ancient Egyptians, had several elements to them, and all were important to their survival in the next world. There were the body, the shadow and the name, and the ka, the ba and the akh. These last three were all forms of the human spirit, and they are almost impossible to translate. The ka is the life force, often called the spirit; the ba has been translated as the soul but is probably more equivalent to personality, and the akh is thought to be the transfigured spirit, possibly the result of the ka and the ba joining in the body after death. In order that this could happen, the physical body had to be preserved if at all possible, and preserved in a recognisable form; this would help the deceased pass into the next world. Mummification had two aims: to preserve the body and to give it a lifelike appearance.

Mummification is one of the most consistent elements of Egyptian culture, beginning in early times and even continuing through the most turbulent periods of Egyptian history. The accidental preservation of human remains in Egypt's dry conditions is considered to have initiated an interest in artificial preservation, which lasted for thousands of years. During the New Kingdom, Egypt's power, strength and wealth meant that more people could afford to be mummified, and there is little difference between non-royal and royal mummies, other than the position of the arms. Kings had their arms crossed over their chests like Osiris. The ritual was the same.

The process of mummification

The corpse would be taken to a 'place of purification', generally on the west bank of the Nile, the side associated with the dead. This site also needed to have a good water supply and be well away from areas where people lived. Here the body was prepared, washed using a natron solution. Natron is a natural salt which has mildly antiseptic properties; it was used to dehydrate the body effectively. Once purified, the body was then taken to the place where it would be embalmed.

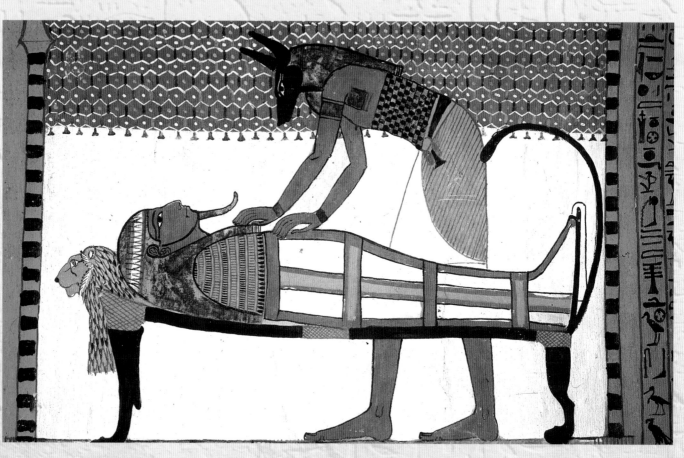

The main priority was to preserve the appearance of the dead person, and the brain was removed – the Egyptians had no idea of its importance – and replaced by material such as resin-soaked linen to keep the shape of the head. The heart, which was thought to be the most important organ, was never removed; other major organs were, through a small incision in the side. These were embalmed separately, dried out, bandaged and put into the canopic jars which would go into the tomb. Then the body was filled with temporary stuffing and covered with natron. Some 40 days later it was uncovered, washed down again, dried, and then given its final filling. It was anointed and the nostrils, ears and mouth would usually be plugged. It might also be decorated and adorned with jewellery. It was then ready to be wrapped.

Bandaging

The bandaging took 15 days. Fingers and toes were wrapped first, individually, and then strips of linen were wound round and round the torso, head and limbs. Sacred amulets were often included in the bandaging. The body had to be as perfect as possible, so if someone had lost a limb in life, for instance, it would be replaced with an artificial one which would also be bandaged. When the process was complete a coat of resin would often be applied and a mask fitted over the body's head and shoulders; Tutankhamun's is the most famous example. The mummified body was now ready to go inside its coffin or, in the case of Tutankhamun and presumably of other kings, in its series of multiple coffins. The whole process took about 70 days in total, during which time all the other preparations for the funeral would have to be made.

Opposite: A painting from the tomb of Sennedjem showing Anubis, the god of embalming, with a mummy. He is about to perform a ceremony known as the Ritual of Osiris.

Above: A plaque would often be placed on the body, covering the incision made to allow the removal of the internal organs; this was then held against the body and wrapped carefully with the bandages. This one, showing the eye of Horus as well as other deities including the jackal-headed Anubis, comes from the tomb of Psusennes I.

Right: Particular care was taken to try and preserve the appearance of the dead person, which is most evident in some of the royal mummies. This is Ramesses II, who was one of Egypt's most powerful rulers and who died at the age of 91.

Howard Carter
and Lord Carnarvon

Howard Carter, later to become one of the most famous archaeologists in the world, was born in London in 1874. His father was an illustrator and animal painter, and Carter inherited his artistic skills. In 1891 his abilities in this area were brought to the attention of Percy Newberry, who was working for the Egypt Exploration Fund, and he used the young Carter to help with work on tracings of scenes from tombs at Beni Hasan. In October that year Carter arrived in Egypt to work at Beni Hasan itself. In 1892 he started working for W.M. Flinders Petrie, the most well-known Egyptologist of his time, but Petrie was not impressed with his archaeological abilities: 'Mr Carter is a good-natured lad,' he wrote, 'whose interest is entirely in painting and natural history'.

Petrie was wrong. Howard Carter's interest in Egyptology was marked, and when he was given the chance to return the following year with the Egypt Exploration Fund as a draughtsman he jumped at it. His new job took him down to Luxor, the site of Thebes, and he worked there for the next six years. He was based on the west bank at Deir el-Bahri, the beautiful 18th Dynasty mortuary temple of the female pharaoh Hatshepsut, where he copied inscriptions and reliefs.

Gaston Maspero, the French Egyptologist, thought more highly of Carter's abilities than Petrie. In 1899 Maspero was reappointed to the post of director of the Egyptian Antiquities Service, and took the opportunity to give him a chance in a more wide-ranging archaeological role. He appointed Carter, who was only in his mid-twenties, as the first Chief Inspector of Antiquities for Upper Egypt. This meant that he had overall responsibility for all the sites at Thebes, as well as elsewhere, including the Valley of the Kings.

Chief Inspector of Upper Egypt

Howard Carter began this new job in January 1900, and one of his first tasks involved working in the Valley. The tomb of Amenhotep II had been found two years previously; it contained 17 royal mummies, in addition to those of the pharaoh for whom it was intended and two members of his immediate family. It had evidently been used in antiquity as a cache for some mummies recovered from other tombs following robberies. Carter had to organise the reinstallation of the king, and of those mummies that were unidentified, and send the rest north to the Giza Museum. He also made his first discovery when he was riding home one evening through the hills west of the Nile as his horse stumbled; it had put one leg in a hole. This turned out to be the entrance to a burial which Carter was able to excavate the following year. Hoping that it would be spectacular, he invited local dignitaries to its opening but it was less than impressive: there was an empty coffin, a statue of King Mentuhotep II (it was linked to his mortuary temple) and a shaft containing some pots and wooden boats. Carter then began fresh work in the Valley, clearing several new tombs, all of which had been plundered.

Howard Carter was typical of a new kind of archaeologist. He believed strongly in conservation and began necessary repair work; he also improved the situation for the visitors the Valley was attracting in increasing numbers. Official funding had to be supplemented and he turned to several rich enthusiasts for sponsorship: Robert Mond, for instance, financed essential restoration work in the tomb of Seti I when the collapse of a pillar threatened the survival of the beautiful night-sky ceiling of the burial chamber. Theodore Davis was another, less easy, sponsor and Carter made several discoveries in the Valley while financed by Davis. The most notable was the tomb of Tuthmosis IV, and shortly afterwards Carter was appointed to a new post, Chief Inspector for Lower Egypt, based in the north of the country.

Carter quits

Howard Carter transferred to Saqqara in 1904. His time in the south had been successful, but he was not the easiest of people; he could be prickly, defensive and abrupt, was rather stubborn, and did not tolerate fools. These characteristics were to bring about the end of his government career.

A group of French tourists were visiting Saqqara in early January 1905 when they tried to see the Serapeum and were told that they needed to buy tickets. At this, some members of the party – who appear to have been very drunk – began to abuse the guards. Eventually they all paid and charged down into the monument, the burial place of sacred bulls, where they discovered an absence of candles. They immediately rushed out again and demanded refunds. At this point Carter was sent for; he did exactly what he was supposed to and declined to give them

their money back. He also told the party to leave. There then followed a scuffle of some kind and the upshot was that the French launched a formal complaint about Carter's behaviour. He seems to have anticipated trouble; he sent a telegraph to the British Consul-General Lord Cromer that very day advising him of what had happened, describing it as an 'affray' and saying that both parties had been 'cut and knocked about'.

Opposite: Portrait of British archaeologist Howard Carter standing next to a cabinet and a birdcage in the early 1920s.

Above: View of the offering chamber of the tomb of Seti I which Carter sought funding to restore.

Left: The mortuary Temple of Hatshepsut in Thebes was where Carter spent six years as a draughtsman.

Carter the freelance

A few unruly, drunken tourists were not going to make Howard Carter give up on Egypt, and he began to eke out a living selling paintings and doing a little dealing in antiquities, a common sideline for many archaeologists at that time. He was a skilled artist and got some commissions, notably one illustrating the finds from the tomb of Yuya and Thuya, but otherwise he relied on selling his work to tourists. He was meticulous and there is evidence that many paintings were discarded as not being of sufficient quality. Things were undoubtedly difficult, and he may have acted as a guide on occasion. In 1907, however, things began to look up when Gaston Maspero did him another favour. A visiting English aristocrat had asked Lord Cromer if he could recommend an archaeologist to help him with his hitherto amateur excavations; Cromer asked Maspero, and Maspero suggested his old protégé and ex-Inspector. Howard Carter was introduced to Lord Carnarvon.

Lord Cromer interviewed Carter, and he was asked to explain what he had done. Condemnation of his behaviour was far from universal but a diplomatic apology was called for to smooth things over. This Carter completely refused to give. He had done his job, acted according to the rules and as he saw best, and he saw no reason why he should need to apologise for anything. He made it clear that if he was pushed to do so he would resign. And then he carried out his threat. This put Maspero, whose appointment Carter had been, in a somewhat difficult position but it did not alter his high opinion of Carter's abilities and he tried, through various unofficial channels, to get him to return. Carter stuck to his guns. Unlike many of the Europeans in Egypt, however, he had no private means to support his enthusiasm for Egyptology – and now he was out of work.

Above: Educated at Eton and Trinity College, Cambridge, Carnarvon had a serious fascination with Egypt and used his vast wealth to finance Carter and the rest of the excavation team, thereby making an enormous contribution to modern archaeology.

Right: An inlaid wooden chest from the tomb of Yuya and Thuya. After leaving Saqqara, Carter, who was a skilled artist, earned money by illustrating finds from the tomb of Yuya and Thuya.

Opposite: An ointment container from the tomb, which had a ritual purpose; the decoration symbolised the king's transformation from childhood through to eventual rebirth. The remains of the original unguents were still present, but they had decayed into a brown, 'bad-smelling' colour.

Lord Carnarvon

George Edward Stanhope Molyneux Herbert, fifth Earl of Carnarvon, was an unlikely candidate for someone who would go on to develop a consuming interest in Egyptology. Seven years older than Howard Carter, he was the epitome of the wealthy English aristocrat; his home – Highclere Castle – was imposing, and he developed a passion for cars. This was, of course, in the early days of motoring, and Carnarvon could not resist speeding. He was prosecuted several times, for travelling at speeds which seem innocuous now, but this did nothing to deter him and, perhaps inevitably, he was involved in a serious accident which took place in Germany in 1901. Carnarvon was hurt but it could have been much worse; his chauffeur had reacted quickly enough to save him from being killed. As it was, the effects were serious and he was badly affected. Never the strongest of men, his health was permanently damaged.

Now in a frail state of health, Carnarvon found the damp, chilly winters intolerable and began to spend them out of England. In 1903 this brought him to Egypt, then a popular wintering place for members of the European upper classes. Though the climate suited him much more, he found the social life tedious and dull and looked around for more congenial ways of spending his time. Egyptology attracted him, and he managed to get a concession to dig in the area of Sheikh Abd el-Qurna. This was granted to him at Lord Cromer's request, but it was not a particularly promising site as it had been much disturbed.

Carnarvon was a complete amateur, utterly inexperienced, and could not have really expected anything with more potential; in fact the site seems to have been deliberately chosen bearing that in mind. Nonetheless he enjoyed it; his dig was quite convenient for the Winter Palace hotel in

Luxor where he based himself during the archaeological season, and he appears to have been content on site. A large tent or cage was made and covered with mosquito netting; Carnarvon sat in it and, protected from both insects and dust, could supervise his excavation in comfort. He was joined by his wife on some occasions, and the overall impression was of a complete amateur playing at archaeology. This was not entirely correct; Carnarvon was serious and enthusiastic even though the site predictably produced nothing more than a mummified cat in a coffin shaped like a crouching feline. Far from being discouraged by this unpromising start, Carnarvon became even more enthralled. The cat was presented to the Cairo Museum.

Enthusiastic amateur he may have been, but he was also realistic and recognised that he simply did not know enough to be taken seriously, and that he was of limited use as an archaeologist. He also knew that this was a factor in the allocation of concessions, and that if he could present a more professional prospect he would probably be granted a concession with greater potential. He needed the help of an experienced Egyptologist, someone with a good track record of excavating in the country. With this in mind he approached Lord Cromer. The British Consul General contacted Gaston Maspero, the head of the Egyptian Antiquities Service, and he suggested Howard Carter.

The two men worked together for many years, generally harmoniously; it seems to have been a genuine meeting of minds. However, their association was cut short by Carnarvon's relatively early death – he was only 57 – from the effects of blood poisoning in April 1923. He had built up a considerable collection of Egyptian antiquities and, by financing Carter's explorations in the Valley of the Kings, made a significant contribution to archaeology.

Working together

With Howard Carter now part of his team, Lord Carnarvon was in a better position. He extended his concession at Thebes, and the results from the west bank of the Nile were immediately good; among other things, Carter found the decorated tomb of an 18th Dynasty mayor. It was an excellent start and in the following years more private tombs were discovered, as were two temples belonging to the reigns of Hatshepsut and Ramesses IV. By 1912 Carter and Carnarvon were ready to look northwards, but their excavations in the Nile delta were less successful; conditions were difficult and the finds not particularly exciting. This did dampen Carnarvon's interest in digging a little and he went back to England. His interest in Egypt did not wane, however, and he continued to build up his collection of antiquities. Carter had suggested that buying artefacts in the bazaars and selling them to other collectors would be a way of defraying some of the expenses, but most seem to have ended up in Carnarvon's own collection. This became one of the finest private collections of Egyptian antiquities and, after his death, was bought by the Metropolitan Museum in New York.

Right from the start, Carter and Carnarvon really wanted to work in the royal valley, but Theodore Davis held that concession and it was initially impossible. In 1914, back in Thebes, Carter had a major success. Artefacts had been appearing

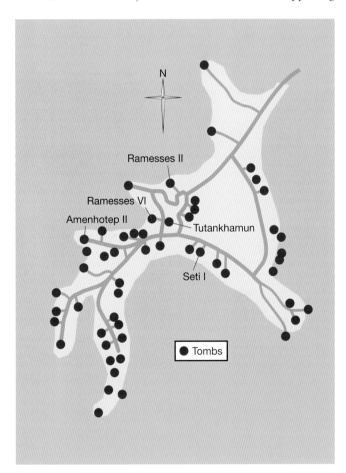

on the local market and it was evident that they had been removed from some as yet undiscovered site. Carter found out what and where it was: a royal tomb that lay just outside the Valley. It may have originally belonged to Amenhotep I and though it had been emptied in antiquity, probably after a robbery, a lot of material had been left behind. Carnarvon was much encouraged by this, the discovery of his first royal tomb. Then the concession he and Carter had been waiting for became available.

The Valley of the Kings

Theodore Davis died in February 1915, but had given up his concession to dig in the Valley shortly beforehand, believing it to be fully explored. By 8 February, Carter was at work there, digging on behalf of Lord Carnarvon and starting with the tomb of Amenhotep III in the western branch, which had hardly been explored. Again this tomb seemed to have been deliberately dismantled, probably between 1000 and 900 BC, and again an assortment of miscellaneous objects had been left behind.

Carnarvon was stranded in England by the First World War and Carter was working as a diplomatic courier as well as an archaeologist. Nonetheless he managed to clear another tomb, built for Hatshepsut before she took the throne, but it had never been used. By 1917 Carter was ready to start work in the main part of the Valley. He had a single aim: finding a tomb which was known to be missing. Davis had looked for it and thought he had found it, but Carter did not believe he had. The tomb he was searching for was that of Tutankhamun. The pharaoh's name was known from inscriptions and some king lists, and he seemed to have ruled for about 10 years during the 18th Dynasty, but no trace had been found of his burial.

Carter's search became systematic and somewhat obsessive – the surface of the Valley was cleared down to the rock in many places and tons of rubble had to be shifted by huge teams of workers. However, finds were not forthcoming. Apart from some calcite jars found by the entrance to the tomb of Merenptah, who succeeded Ramesses II, almost nothing was discovered. It was not only deeply discouraging, it was also using an enormous amount of money. Lord Carnarvon was beginning to swing round to Davis's view that all the tombs in the Valley had already been found.

Opposite: The Valley of the Kings, well away from inhabited areas in the time of the New Kingdom when it was established, may well have been intended to provide some protection for the tombs located within it.

Opposite above: English Egyptologist Howard Carter (1874–1939, right) walks with the patron of his research, archaeologist and Fifth Earl, Lord Carnarvon (1866–1923), at the Valley of the Kings excavation site, Egypt.

Right: A gold statuette of Amun-Re which became the focus of Lord Carnarvon's collection. It was apparently found in 1916 by Howard Carter, north of the temple of Karnak; Carter thought it might have been 18th Dynasty in date, but it is now thought to be more recent, perhaps dating from about 900 BC.

The Discovery

By the winter of 1921–2, Lord Carnarvon was becoming disillusioned with work in the Valley. The excavations were expensive – a hand-propelled railway had been installed to help move the masses of debris that Carter's work was generating – and there was little to show for it. There was certainly no sign of the missing pharaoh, and Carnarvon decided it was time to abandon the search. He asked Carter to come and see him at Highclere Castle, and they reviewed their work. Then Carnarvon broke the news that he could no longer afford to finance what seemed to have become a hunt after shadows. Carter, who was equally disappointed and equally realistic, had been expecting this decision but he had a plan, essentially a bet which he hoped the Earl would be unable to resist.

Carnarvon still held the concession, and Carter offered to pay for one last season himself. There was one patch of ground that still had to be investigated properly, an area near the entrance to the tomb of Ramesses IV; he had partly been avoiding it due to the inconvenience digging would cause. There were also some workmen's huts, dating to the Ramessid period, which would need to be demolished. Carter suggested excavating this area, and said that anything he found would belong to Carnarvon as holder of the concession. Carnarvon took the bait – and, impressed by Carter's conviction, agreed to finance this last season himself.

The 'Last Season'

Howard Carter arrived back in Luxor on 28 October, and began recruiting workmen immediately. On Wednesday 1 November he started work on the designated patch of land, just by the tomb of Ramesses IV. It would have been difficult for him to be optimistic; Edward Ayrton had worked near there for Theodore Davis in 1905–6 and Carter himself had explored the area briefly in 1920; foundation deposits had been found and the workmen's huts revealed. But Carter wanted to investigate the area again because no one had dug below the level of the huts. By 3 November these had been excavated, planned and fully recorded; they were then to be removed. Beneath them the surface soil would also have to be stripped away.

Something out of the ordinary...

Carter's own account records what happened on 4 November. 'Hardly had I arrived at work the next morning than the unusual silence, due to the stoppage of the work, made me realise that something out of the ordinary had happened, and I was greeted by the announcement that a step cut in the rock had been discovered underneath the very first hut to be attacked…'.

By 5 November all the rubbish had been moved and the upper edges of the stair could be seen. Clearing work began and Carter watched apprehensively as the steps were gradually

through which he could shine his torch, and found that the passage on the other side of the door seemed to be full of rubble. Anything could lie beyond. The basic design seemed compatible with an 18th Dynasty date, but the entrance was small; it could be the tomb of a courtier or a cache, a place where royal mummies had been hidden for safety. Carter closed the small hole in the door and the steps were filled in for protection. The workmen were as excited as he was, and he selected some to guard the place. He finally went home, knowing that he could – for the moment – do no more.

Carnarvon was still in England and the next morning Carter sent him a cable: 'At last have made wonderful discovery in Valley, a magnificent tomb with seals intact, recovered same for your arrival, congratulations.' Back in the Valley, the excavation was filled to surface level and the boulders which had made up the workmen's huts were rolled over the top to await Carnarvon; word that something had been found was beginning to spread.

Carnarvon and his daughter Evelyn arrived in Luxor on 23 November and by the afternoon of the following day the entire staircase had been cleared. Most of the blocked door was now visible and towards the bottom the seal impressions were particularly clear. Among them were ones giving the name of Tutankhamun.

An intact tomb?

Despite this, it was still not clear what would lie behind the door. Now that almost all of it could be seen it was obvious that it had, at some point, been opened and resealed – and not just once, but twice. The first seals that Carter had found, the royal necropolis

revealed one by one. They seemed likely to lead to a tomb, but it could be an unfinished one or one that had been plundered. The steps descended under the slope of the rock, gradually becoming covered until they were effectively in a passage, then – at the level of the twelfth – the top of a doorway was revealed. It was solid, blocked and plastered, and the plaster was marked by the impression of seals. The seal used was the jackal with nine captives, the official seal of the royal necropolis. Carter was looking at the closed and sealed doorway of, quite possibly, a royal tomb.

It was near the end of the day, but Carter could not resist searching what could be seen of the door for any other seals, ones which might reveal the name of the tomb's owner. He was unsuccessful, but the use of the necropolis seal meant that the tomb had belonged to a very important individual, even if not a pharaoh. Some plaster had fallen from the top of the door, and Carter spotted a wooden lintel. He made a small hole below it

Opposite: In the foreground left is the entrance to the tomb of Ramesses IX. Tutankhamun's tomb entrance can be seen midground to the right.

Above: George Herbert, Fifth Earl of Carnarvon and his daughter Evelyn.

Right: Looking back up the passage into Tutankhamun's tomb to the steps at the entrance. The passage was packed with rubble, some of it including fragile and valuable artefacts.

seal of the jackal and nine captives, had been applied to the resealed part. Tutankhamun's name was on the lower, original part, so the tomb had probably belonged to him – but what had happened since? Carter knew that whatever it was, it could not have taken place later than the 20th Dynasty because of the huts which had been built above, and which had not been disturbed since their construction.

Sorting through the debris that had filled the stairway deepened the mystery. There were broken pieces of pots and boxes, and the latter bore a variety of names: Akhenaten, Smenkhkare, Tutankhamun. To confuse the picture even further a fragment with Amenhotep III's name was found, as was a scarab of Tuthmosis III. The mixture of names suggested that they might be looking at a cache rather than a burial, and if it was a cache, then the royal mummies it included would – on previous evidence – probably have been extensively damaged by robbers.

Clearing the passage

By the morning of 25 November the door was completely clear. All the seals were carefully recorded and the plastered blocks were removed. Behind lay a passage, sloping downwards. It was packed with rubble and this also showed signs of having been disturbed: most was limestone, which Carter described as 'clean white chip',

Above: Howard Carter emerges from the entrance of Tutankhamun's tomb with a tray of numbered artefacts.

Right: Against the west wall of the Antechamber were stacked three ceremonial couches of extraordinary fineness and beauty. Behind the bundles stacked under this one was found the hidden entrance to the Annexe.

but part had been packed with flint. A tunnel seemed to have been quarried through the infill in the upper left-hand side, matching the patched hole in the doorway, and had then been refilled. Work began on emptying the passage. It went slowly because the main part of the rubble included many delicate items and fragments, all representing evidence of a robbery. By the end of the day they had progressed some way down the passage, but there was no sign of a door.

The following day, 26 November, was to be one of the most momentous in the history of archaeology, though they excavators had little inkling of this; they were now firmly convinced it would be a cache. The delicate work of clearing the passage continued and by mid-afternoon they had reached another doorway. This was also sealed, again with seals of both the royal necropolis and Tutankhamun, and also showed signs of having been breached and resealed at some point. The last of the debris was cleared from the door.

As with the first entrance, Carter made a small opening in the upper left-hand corner. He inserted a testing rod to see if there was rubble behind this door too, but there was evidently a void. He withdrew the rod and tested for bad air with a candle. Everything was all right so he widened the hole, inserted the candle and peered in. 'At first I could see nothing,' he wrote later, 'the hot air escaping from the chamber, but presently, as my eyes grew accustomed to the light, details of the room within emerged slowly from the mist, strange animals, statues, and everywhere the glint of gold.' Thunderstruck by what he saw, he was unable to speak, and behind him Carnarvon had to ask if Carter could see anything. 'Yes,' Carter managed to say, 'wonderful things.'

Treasure for the Afterlife

Eventually the hole was widened, and Carter and Carnarvon clambered down into the room they had found, accompanied by Carnarvon's daughter Lady Evelyn Herbert and Arthur Callender, a friend and colleague of Carter whose engineering expertise would soon be invaluable. They stood in the gloom, dumbfounded and surrounded by apparently chaotic heaps of treasure, where no one had been for over 3000 years.

Opposite them were three tall gilt couches, shaped like elongated animals with long legs. Even today they are surprising; picked out from the surrounding darkness in torch beams they were unearthly. Two life-size statues of the king stood to their right, facing each other either side of an area of wall which seemed to be another blocked door; the light glittered off the golden kilts, headdresses, jewellery, staffs and even sandals worn by the figures. Then they began to notice other things: exquisite chests; alabaster vases; a magnificent inlaid golden throne; a pile of strange white containers under one of the large couches; a confused heap of what appeared to be chariot parts. But it was getting late and they had to go; exploration could start the following day.

Callender swiftly installed electric lighting which actually seemed to increase the air of unreality, and in the first few days they were able to get an idea of the tomb's layout. There was

indeed a sealed entrance between the two life-size guardian statues, and beneath the furthermost couch was an entrance to another chamber. The excavators called the first room they entered the Antechamber, and this second one became the Annexe. The door between the two statues had also been resealed in antiquity and it was breached discreetly (the room beyond would be officially 'opened' later). It led into the Burial Chamber, and Carter, Carnarvon and Lady Evelyn managed to squeeze in; the space was almost entirely filled with a huge golden shrine. At one end of the shrine was an opening into another chamber, which they called the Treasury.

The exceptional scale of the discovery was immediately apparent, and a specialist, multi-disciplinary team was assembled, a contrast to the way much Egyptology had been done in the past. It was the beginning of a long and complicated job that would last for many years, and it all centred around one person: the boy pharaoh Tutankhamun.

Above: Howard Carter, left, and Arthur Callender, right, at work in the Antechamber, meticulously packaging up the artefacts found there. At this point one of the two guardian statues found by the sealed entrance to the Burial Chamber can be seen packaged on the porter's tray to the right while its companion stands against the end wall to the left.

The Afterlife

Grave goods, objects like flint knives or storage jars, have been found in some of the very earliest Ancient Egyptian burials. The presence of these basic, everyday items seems to indicate a belief in some sort of life after death in which they would be needed. What these early beliefs were is uncertain because there is no written evidence. Once that appears, the complexity of Ancient Egyptian concepts of the Afterlife becomes evident. They believed strongly that they could gain eternal life by following a series of actions, from providing funerary equipment to expressing their religious belief and piety. Specific details of beliefs changed and developed over time, but the core remained.

Funerary texts have often been found, buried with the dead, or painted or carved on the walls of tombs. From these we know that the world of the Afterlife was somewhere in the heavens and that the dead ascended into it; the journey was perilous as many dangerous obstacles could block the way. One of the purposes of the funerary texts was to provide the dead with a guide to possible routes and give them the spells which had to be uttered at specific points. The journey could be made upwards in many ways, from riding on the back of a bird or using a reed boat to being wafted up on waves of incense. Once the journey had been completed the deceased could expect to find themselves in the next world.

The Afterworld

The Afterworld was very similar to the valley of the Nile, but perfect. Fields were watered by brimming channels; there were all the necessities of life, but in abundance. Tomb paintings often depict the owner and his wife working in the fields of the Afterworld, sometimes incongruously dressed in their best clothes. They would certainly not have actually expected to do this – or they would have hoped not to – as tombs also contained shabti figures. People who could afford to do so made sure that they went into the Afterlife generously equipped, and shabtis were part of this. They were miniature figures of helpers, and rich and royal tombs could contain hundreds. Some have implements like hoes – and they might be accompanied by overseer-shabtis with whips – and they were supposed to do any menial work which might be required. They often have inscriptions written on them, extracts from funerary texts which make their duties quite clear.

Entry to the Afterworld

In the Afterworld, the deceased would be closer to the gods, but admission was no certainty. A life would be assessed in a ceremony of judgement called the 'Weighing of the Heart' which took place before the god Osiris. The heart of the dead person was balanced against the feather of Maat, the goddess of truth, and the deceased also had to swear that he or she had not committed any of a long list of crimes and offences. Those who failed this test simply ceased to exist, a terrifying prospect for Ancient Egyptians.

Mummification could improve the chances of entering the Afterworld, but it wasn't an absolute necessity; only the most important members of society could afford such an elaborate and expensive ritual. Dying with a 'virtuous heart' was, however, essential. In addition, continuing life in the Afterworld had to be ensured, and the survival of an individual's name was one of the ways this could be achieved. This is one of the reasons why, for example, the name of the heretical pharoah Akhenaten was often chipped out of inscriptions.

A king like Tutankhamun would not just live an ideal life in the Afterworld, as his subjects would hope to do. The king seems to have been thought of as becoming one with the gods, almost as though he became another aspect of Osiris when he died. He also became one with the heavens and the earth in some way, though he still had his individuality. This paradox is still unclear, but it is evident in most of the royal tombs.

Opposite: The god Anubis weighing the heart of a dead man against the truth – the feather of the goddess Maat – in a depiction of the 'Weighing of the Heart' ritual which had to be undergone before admission to the Afterworld.

Above: This small shabti, designed to labour in the Afterworld in place of the deceased, is from the tomb of the 19th Dynasty pharaoh Seti I.

Right: The deceased would lead an ideal life in the next world, and it is this that is depicted in tomb paintings. These dancers and musicians reflect the life the tomb owner, an official called Nebamun, hoped he would enjoy. They wear cones of perfumed ointment on their heads.

The World of Tutankhamun

Until his tomb was found, Tutankhamun remained a ruler familiar only to scholars and specialists. But the period in which he lived was extraordinary, and his burial bears witness to the splendour of Egypt during his time.

Tutankhamun's Egypt

The New Kingdom, into which Tutankhamun was born, was a period of great prosperity for Egypt, but it arose out of a phase of occupation and war. The Middle Kingdom, which ran from c.2055–1650 BC, had been a time of peace and general security, and had seen Egypt's rulers first attempt to extend their influence abroad. It is thought that many people from western Asia may have settled in the area of the Delta as a result of this, though there may also have been an element of incursion; however they came to be in Egypt, their influence was massive. The ruling Dynasty began to fail, and these people took over. They are known as the Hyksos, and Hyksos kings formed the 15th and 16th Dynasties.

The struggle against the Hyksos

Though this occupation is often seen as a complete disaster for Egypt, there do seem to have been some benefits, such as the introduction of improved military equipment like the horse-drawn chariot and the composite bow, and an increased skill in working metal, notably bronze. The lyre and the vertical loom could also have been Hyksos introductions. However, for the first time in its history Egypt was ruled by foreigners.

Around Thebes in the south of the country an Egyptian Dynasty of rulers arose, apparently as vassals to the Hyksos. One king of this Dynasty, the 17th, finally rebelled and started a campaign with the aim of driving the Hyksos out. The evidence is confusing, but the body of this ruler, Seqenenre Taa, was found in a cache of royal mummies at Deir el-Bahri. He had received horrific head injuries which seemed to have been made with an axe, perfectly compatible with a bronze Hyksos weapon. The next king was Kamose, followed by his brother Ahmose, and they achieved what Seqenenre Taa had died attempting to do – the expulsion of the Hyksos from Egypt.

The New Kingdom

Ahmose became the first ruler of both the New Kingdom and the 18th Dynasty. He and his successors consolidated their position, creating what was effectively a buffer state of smaller protectorates in western Asia, governed by rulers who owed their allegiance to the pharaoh. They also colonised Nubia to the south, using a combination of diplomacy and war, and so began the creation of the Egyptian Empire. This was an empire with access to vast sources of wealth, especially after the campaigns of one of the greatest warrior kings, Tuthmosis III. He extended Egyptian control in the Levant, and the spoils of his campaigns were enormous. By 1447 BC he was receiving presents from Babylon and Assyria, a large quantity of lead and copper from Cyprus and silver from the Hittite empire. Booty – tribute, essentially – continued to flow in, increasing the wealth and power of Egypt even further. By the time Tuthmosis III died, his empire stretched from the fourth cataract of the Nile, in what is now Sudan, northwards as far as the Euphrates.

The kings of the 18th Dynasty had originated from the area of Thebes, and that city had a new significance. Though Amun had originally been a local Theban god, his importance had gradually increased in the Middle Kingdom. Now, under Theban rulers, he became the most prominent god in the Ancient Egyptian state. His Theban temple at Karnak grew enormously throughout the New Kingdom but Thebes was by now more than a religious centre; it was also an administrative base. Memphis, in the north, remained important – it was not easy to control the empire, and indeed the country, from the southern centre – but the emphasis seems to have shifted at intervals. Rulers, and presumably their courts, moved between the two, and many high officials built their tombs at Memphis rather than Thebes even though the New Kingdom rulers were buried in the south, in the Valley of the Kings.

The king and the god Amun

The king was central. Not only was he a god-king, but he also had ultimate control of the centralised administration of the state. There were many senior officials, of course: viceroys of Nubia, viziers, generals, state treasurers, mayors of important towns. There were also the high priests, especially the high priest of Amun, whose power grew with the power of his god. Much of the wealth coming into Egypt found its way to Karnak, the centre of the cult of Amun, and the priesthood there became the wealthiest body in Egypt apart from the king.

There is some evidence that the kings who followed Tuthmosis III were beginning to see this as a threat. During the reign of his grandson Tuthmosis IV, another cult began to grow in importance, a revived cult of the sun. It may have been developed in part to counteract the overwhelming power of Amun and his priests; another factor could have been that by identifying himself with the sun the king could stress his watch over all the lands Egypt controlled. It could also have been due to Tuthmosis's personal piety. Whatever the reasons were, there were to be wide-ranging consequences.

Amenhotep III

The next ruler was Amenhotep III who came to the throne at a time of unsurpassed wealth and influence for Egypt. Gifts from other rulers poured in – not just precious objects and valuable

Opposite: Amun's temple at Karnak, reflected in the water of the sacred lake of the complex. Karnak grew massively during the New Kingdom, but most people would not have seen inside; entrance was normally restricted to those with a priestly role.

Left: The Hypostyle Hall of the great temple of Amun at Karnak, built by the 19th Dynasty ruler Seti I, originally had 134 immense columns supporting the roof. As light only came in at the very top, it would have been gloomy.

materials, but also princesses for the royal harem – and the empire was strong. Amenhotep took a woman named Tiye as his principal wife – 'Great Royal Wife' was her title; there is no equivalent word to queen – who was not of royal blood. Her parents were a couple named Yuya and Thuya, whose tomb was discovered in the Valley of the Kings in 1905. Though they were not members of the royal family, they are now thought to have had a lot of influence during the reign of Amenhotep's father. Yuya and Thuya had at least one other child, a son called Anen who was a priest of Amun, and there is a possibility that Ay, who came to the throne after Tutankhamun's death, may also have been their son.

Queen Tiye seems to have wielded real power. Her name is written in a cartouche like that of the king, which is unusual,

and she is sometimes depicted in a kingly way: seated on a throne or shown as a sphinx trampling over the enemies of Egypt. She and Amenhotep had at least six children, two sons and four daughters. The king had other wives, several of whom were those foreign princesses, and also married some of his daughters. It used to be thought that incest in the Egyptian royal family was due to the right of succession passing down the female side, but this is not now thought to be the case. The gods married immediate family members, and it is believed the royal family did the same to emphasise the link between themselves and the gods, as well as stressing their exclusivity and difference.

In the early part of Amenhotep III's reign the major centre of power was Memphis, though no trace of his palace has been found there. Later on the family's main residence seems to

have been Thebes and the palace he built at Malkata on the west bank; it was certainly associated with two major jubilee festivals. The Malkata palace was extensive, and included an enormous artificial lake. Egypt was peaceful, the heart of a strong empire; its wealth was immense and the overall impression is that life, for many people, was good.

The old sun cult which had begun to show signs of developing under Tuthmosis IV grew further under his son. There were many aspects of the sun, and Amenhotep III appears to have built a sanctuary to one, Re-Horakty, in the temple at Karnak. He may have intended to link the older cult to that of Amun or he may have intended to subtly diminish the power of Amun; it may have been deliberately provocative. Amenhotep also began to stress the importance of another aspect of the sun:

the Aten, the sun disc itself. This soon became crucial, but Amenhotep may simply have been using the name as a synonym for Re-Horakty. His son, however, would elevate the Aten to a position of immense importance, causing an enormous rift with the priesthood of Amun and profoundly affecting Egypt.

Above: Tiye, the wife of Amenhotep III, the daughter of Yuga and Thuya who – though not of royal blood themselves – were buried in the Valley of the Kings.

Opposite: Tomb paintings portrayed an ideal New Kingdom world, but for people like Nakht – from whose tomb comes this illustration of noble ladies feasting while accompanied by a blind harpist – life must have been comfortable. Nakht was an official during the riegn of Tuthmosis IV, the father of Amenhotep III.

Above: There are many statues of Amenhotep III, Tutankhamun's grandfather, and other remains from his reign, and a lot of the representations of the king have a distinctive appearance. The Colossi of Memnon, two gigantic statues almost 18 metres high, were built by him to stand at the entrance of his mortuary temple at Thebes.

Akhenaten

Tiye and Amenhotep III's eldest son was called Tuthmosis. He died, however, and his place was taken by his younger brother, another Amenhotep. Scholars have long argued about whether Amenhotep IV became king after his father's death or whether there was a period of joint kingship and, if so, how long it lasted; there is still no clear answer and the debates still rage. Amenhotep IV is the most controversial ruler Egypt ever had, dividing opinion to this day, and he is now better known by the name he took part of the way into his reign: Akhenaten.

At the beginning of his reign Amenhotep IV started building at Karnak in the great temple of Amun. Kings had a duty to build temples – it was an essential part of the relationship they had with the gods – and Amenhotep IV facilitated the process by building with smaller blocks than was the norm, blocks which could be carried by a single worker. However, his temples in the main precinct of the temple at Karnak were not dedicated to Amun but to the sun disc Aten, which the king saw as the sole creator of life. This was a major change, and his queen Nefertiti was also given a prominent role in the carved reliefs – another difference.

Changes in artistic styles

Artistic changes were taking place as well. The royal styles of both Amenhotep IV's father and grandfather, Amenhotep III and

Tuthmosis IV, had begun to change – the standard representation of the pharaoh as an ideal, though still human, man had been replaced by an increasingly unearthly appearance – but under their successor the change was extraordinary. Not only was a lot of the art much more informal, but the king and queen, and other members of the royal family, were also shown with a peculiarly distorted body shape. They have long, narrow faces, especially pronounced in representations of the king; elongated skulls; sagging bellies; spindly lower parts to both legs and arms but exaggerated, wide thighs and hips; narrow shoulders and, in the case of the king, pronounced breasts. There are two main theories about why this change happened, and they could both be true. The first is that the art reflects the king's actual appearance, that other family members were simply shown in the same way, and that he may have suffered from some illness or disorder such as Marfan's syndrome, which is genetic. The other interpretation is that the radical changes in art were linked to the equally radical changes in theology, and that they were intended to stress the 'otherness' of the royal family. This may also have been the reason behind the change in the way Akhenaten's father and grandfather were shown.

Amenhotep Becomes Akhenaten

Everything seems to have come to a head about five to seven years into Amenhotep IV's reign. The cult of the Aten became increasingly important and the king changed his name to Akhenaten, which translates as 'transfigured spirit of the Aten'. He decided to leave Thebes, heartland of the cult of Amun, and establish a new centre dedicated to the Aten. His city, now known as Amarna, was in Middle Egypt, many miles from both Thebes and Memphis. It was named Akhetaten, 'horizon of the Aten', and was laid out east of the Nile. The boundaries were marked by carved stones – stelae – in the cliffs around the crescent-shaped site and the town was apparently planned around the location's symbolic significance. Because Amarna was abandoned shortly after Akhenaten's death and never rebuilt, archaeological digs have revealed a lot about it, and continue to do so. It was in this place that Tutankhamun is likely to have been born.

Opposite: This relief of Akhenaten, his wife Nefertiti and three children came from a private house at Amarna and may have formed part of a shrine. The Aten, the sun disc, shines down on the royal family. Their oldest daughter Meritaten is being kissed by her father, while Meketaten is on her mother's knee. The child on her shoulder is Ankhesenpaaten, who would become Tutankhamun's queen.

Left: The way Akhenaten was portrayed changed during his reign; in many statues and carvings his features and the shape of his body are almost bizarre and quite distinctive. In this depiction of the king with his wife Nefertiti he is much more 'normal' in appearance.

Akhenaten's city

The population of Akhenaten's city has been estimated at somewhere between 20,000 and 50,000; the surrounding area could easily have supported one of some 45,000 people. Tombs, both private ones and those for members of the royal family, were constructed in the surrounding cliffs. Many discoveries have been made there, from details that reveal aspects of everyday life (going by the piles of domestic refuse found, rubbish must have been a problem) to great artistic treasures, such as the famous portrait bust of Queen Nefertiti, and invaluable state archives. There is a gradual variation in house sizes which suggests that this was not a place with sharp differences between rich and poor, but rather one with a smooth gradation between people of different social standing. There was one huge difference, however: between the royal family and the rest of the population. That difference was even reinforced.

There were many state buildings, including two main temples of the Aten and a building known as the King's House which had a 'window of appearances' overlooking an open courtyard. Members of the royal family would make formal appearances here, and it is the place from which Akhenaten

rewarded deserving officials by throwing down necklaces for them. There was another big complex of buildings, originally dubbed the Great Palace but now thought to have had a religious function. To the north lay a royal palace, the North Palace. This was a walled compound; rooms and courtyards were arranged around a pool, and in one corner was a sunken garden. This was surrounded by columns and small rooms which had walls decorated with naturalistic scenes of birds in thickets of papyrus. Another room in this palace had walls which were decorated with more paintings, but all over: unusual as most Egyptian wall decoration only covered part of the wall. From inscriptions that have been found there, it looks as though the North Palace was used by the women of the royal family.

Akenaten's religion

Initially, at least, Akhenaten's new cult was able to fit in with the old religion. The Egyptian pantheon of gods had always altered over time, with new deities being incorporated and the importance of many of them shifting, either increasing or diminishing. Akhenaten's views seem to have become more extreme as time went on, and a compromise was no longer possible; eventually he demanded a complete rejection of the old order. The name of Amun was removed from monuments throughout Egypt, though this was haphazard in some places, and temples were closed. Offerings were diverted to the Aten

cult, which had the incidental benefit of making the king – so closely identified with the cult that the Aten could only be worshipped through him – immensely wealthy. Property which had been confiscated from the cult of Amun was now administered by government officials rather than priests. Many of these men, the courtiers of the new regime, seem to have been protégés of the king who owed their positions to his patronage, rather than being members of the old elite. Some people adapted their names, changing the now-inappropriate '-amun' elements to '-aten', which would have been politic for anyone who wished to prosper under Akhenaten's rule.

Akhenaten's own position was made as unassailable as possible. He emphasised his divine role by identifying himself strongly with the Aten, becoming the human manifestation of his god. Only he could proclaim the will of his father the Aten, and only he could determine what it was. It was, in many ways, a continuation of the position of the king under the old regime, but in a much exaggerated form – and with only one god, and with only Akhenaten and Nefertiti as mediators, people seem to have been obliged to worship the king and queen. The removal

of the old gods must have been extremely difficult for many people. Perhaps the absence of the old state gods would not have made much difference in everyday life, but to face something as perilous as childbirth, for example, without the protection of the god Bes or without the goddesses Hathor, Hekmet and Taweret to invoke, would have been a very different matter.

Opposite above: A partly completed relief of an Amarna princess – exactly which of the six daughters of Akhenaten and Nefertiti is unclear – eating. Such intimate portrayals of members of the royal family only occur in the Amarna period.

Opposite below: The famous painted limestone bust of Nefertiti was found at Amarna in what appears to have been the studio of Thutmose, the royal sculptor; it may have been used as a model or to train other craftsmen.

Above: The Amarna royal family worshipping the Aten, whose rays shine down towards them. This particular carving still has traces of the original colour.

The Gods

The gods were central to the prosperity and even the survival of Egypt: they protected the land and the people. The pharaoh derived his power from them, and in many ways he formed a bridge between the gods and the rest of humanity, and could mediate between them. Temples were an aspect of this: the ruler built temples and made sure that offerings were given to the gods, and in return the gods enabled Egypt to flourish.

Priests acted on the pharaoh's behalf, and religion and daily life were deeply linked. It was important to make sure that the state was stable and that the people continued to prosper, both in the short and long term – that the next harvest would be a good one, for example, but also that future generations would benefit from such blessings. Only the gods could ensure this.

Scenes from temples and tombs, surviving papyri and other documents can help in the understanding of Egyptian religion, but there does not seem to have been a single work, an Ancient Egyptian equivalent of the Bible or the Koran, which defined it. There are many versions of the creation story, for instance, and it is impossible to say when the worship of particular deities started. There were lots of gods and goddesses in the Egyptian pantheon, many of whom could take different forms and have different 'responsibilities'. There were deities of universal importance, like Osiris, Isis and Horus, and there were ones whose areas of interest were more limited, either to a specific place or to a particular role or trade. The emphasis could sometimes shift: the god Amun had originally been a relatively local god in Thebes, but developed into the king of all the gods.

The differing roles some deities had can be shown by three examples. Isis, the wife of Osiris, was a very important goddess; she represented magic and was in some ways the divine mother of the king. Osiris had more aspects. He was the god of the dead and was therefore closely associated with the Afterlife, but also with rebirth, fertility and, by extension, farming and cultivation. Hathor, another very important goddess, also had a divine maternal role, but was linked to love, sexuality and fertility, music, dance, alcohol – and was also the 'Lady of the West', important in the Afterlife.

Representing the gods

When it came to representing these gods, certain standard conventions were followed, often respecting the form the gods or goddesses might take in a particular role. Hathor, depending on her particular aspect, could be shown as a cow, a woman with cow's ears, or horns with a sun disc, or with a falcon standing on a perch balanced on her head. Isis was comparatively straightforward, usually depicted as a woman wearing a specific type of headdress. Osiris was illustrated as a mummified man, holding a crook and flail on his chest. Amun could be a kingly man wearing a tall double-plume headdress, a ram-headed man, or just be shown as a ram; he could also be frog-headed or depicted as a goose. Some forms were more common than others and some gods, like Anubis the god of embalming, were more consistent – he is always shown either as a jackal or as a man with a jackal's head.

Tutankhamun's tomb

The gods, and their symbols, are everywhere. In Tutankhamun's tomb there are straightforward representations, such as the large figure of Anubis as a jackal or the wall paintings illustrating the king's arrival in the underworld, where he is greeted by several deities, including Hathor with her falcon symbol on her head. There were also many items with a more obscure meaning – obscure nowadays, but they would have been clear to Tutankhamun's contemporaries. The jewellery had symbolic aspects, for instance: a ring with an eye on it actually shows the eye of Horus, which symbolically depicted wholeness, perfection and strength, but also healing. Then there are those items described as 'cult objects' or 'magical objects', at whose significance we can only guess, such as the two strange 'Anubis

fetishes'. These each show a headless animal body, which is mostly limbless but otherwise intact, hanging upside down from a staff which is set in a conical base. Whatever their form, the gods were everywhere.

Opposite: A bronze statuette of the goddess Maat from the 16th Dynasty. Maat represented truth, the way things should be, and could also be represented by her symbolic feather. Here this is shown on her head.

Above: Ram-headed sphinxes from the great temple of the god Amun at Karnak. Among other things, Amun could be depicted as a ram, a ram-headed human, or as a kingly man; he was the ruler of the gods.

The Life of Tutankhamun

Akhenaten and his queen Nefertiti had six daughters. The eldest was Meritaten, then came Meketaten, followed by Ankhesenpaaten who was born in about his seventh year as ruler. The final three appear to have died in childhood, and not much more is known about them other than their names, but

Left: The most significant change during Tutankhamun's reign was the restoration of the old religion, and the abandonment of both Akhenaten's cult of the Aten and his city of Amarna. Here Tutankhamun is shown in the company of the reinstated god Amun.

Ankhesenpaaten was married to someone who ensured that she would become the most familiar. Her husband was Tutankhamun.

Who was Tutankhamun?

Despite the fact that Tutankhamun is now the most famous of Egypt's rulers very little is actually known about him. He was of royal blood, but his exact parentage is unknown. It was long assumed that if Akhenaten had actually had a son then the boy would have been shown on monuments, like his sisters, but throughout the 18th Dynasty there is a general absence of prince's names on their father's monuments. Tutankhamun is, however, mentioned on a stone block which probably came from Amarna, and where he is described as 'the son of the King, of his own body' and given his original name of Tutankhaten. He is likely to have been brought up in Akhenaten's city, where objects bearing his name have been found. Another possible father is Amenhotep III, but this suggestion is less likely as there would have had to be a long co-regency for the older king to have been Tutankhamun's parent. So today it is widely thought that Akhenaten was indeed Tutankhamun's father, but that Nefertiti was not his mother. She was not Akhenaten's only wife, and a likely candidate is the Lady Kiya. She was favoured by the king in the middle of his reign, but disappears after year 11; this was about the time that Tutankhamun was born, and Kiya may have died in childbirth. One of the supporting pieces of evidence is a relief illustrating a scene of mourning for someone who appears to have just given birth, and the baby is being fanned: a sign of royal status.

Tutankhamun's reign

When Tutankhaten succeeded to the throne he was a child, probably about 8 or 9. Governance of Egypt would have been in the hands of others, mainly his principal advisor Ay, but also Horemheb, who was in charge of the army. The young ruler was persuaded to return the country to the old religion, and the names of the king and queen were altered to reflect this; they became Tutankhamun and Ankhesenamun. Early in the reign the court left Amarna, and was once again established in Memphis and Thebes. There is some evidence of military campaigns – Horemheb seems to have been reasserting Egyptian authority in western Asia and possibly Nubia – but the return to religious orthodoxy would mark Tutankhamun's reign as significant even without the discovery of his tomb. Restoration and repair work was carried out, though the credit for much of this was usurped by his successors, and new monuments were also built.

The end of Amarna

The end of Akhenaten's reign is clouded in confusion and speculation. His religious zeal escalated and temples to all gods other than the Aten were suppressed; the political situation in western Asia appears to have been disintegrating. There also seem to have been many deaths in the royal family – certainly some people, including Nefertiti, vanish from the record (though she may have changed her name). There is confusion, too, about Smenkhkare, a mysterious individual who was co-ruler with Akhenaten right at the end of his reign. He could be another son of Akhenaten's, possibly also by Kiya, or he could be a younger brother, or some scholars believe the name was used by Nefertiti. In 1907 a burial was found in the Valley of the Kings which contained a male body in a damaged coffin: all the names had been obliterated. The deceased was closely related to Tutankhamun – they share a distinctive skull shape and a relatively uncommon blood group – and this could be Akhenaten or the elusive Smenkhkare. Determining the body's age would settle matters but, yet again, the evidence is unclear.

Above left: One of the four calcite stoppers from the canopic chest found in Tutankhamun's tomb which held his mummified internal organs. The realism is heightened by the red pigment applied to the lips. It may well be a portrait.

Right: Statuette of Amenhotep III, who is thought to be the grandfather of Tutankhamun.

Tutankhamun and his Court

The Egyptian state was focused on the pharaoh, but the day-to-day running of the Egyptian empire was overseen by a number of officials – and during Tutankhamun's minority, these men would effectively have run the country. Tutankhamun was at the top of the pyramid of Egyptian society, and his contact with the details of government would have been limited even when he became old enough. Two of his most senior courtiers became pharaoh in their turn, and there were others of whom we know a little, on two occasions because they presented items for inclusion among his grave goods. As with many aspects of Tutankhamun's life, a lot of information is missing.

Ay – 'The God's Father'

Ay was the most senior member of the court. His precise relationship to Tutankhamun remains in doubt as he left no details of his parentage or children in his own tomb, and there has been much speculation. He used the title 'The God's Father' as part of his name, but that reflects his central political importance rather than a physical relationship. Ay does seem to have been related to the royal family, however, and it has been suggested that he might have been Nefertiti's father – or many other things. Whatever the reality, he appears to have had close links to the royal house, both at Amarna and then back in Thebes following the death of Akhenaten.

As Tutankhamun's principal adviser, Ay would have controlled access to the young king and, as a result, he wielded considerable power. There has been some speculation that Ay may have murdered Tutankhamun but this looks unlikely; he did, however, follow him as pharaoh. He was elderly when he came to the throne and only ruled for four years. His decorated tomb has been found in the Valley of the Kings but all that remains of its contents are a few fragments of gold foil found in another burial. The paintings in Ay's tomb are so similar in style to those in Tutankhamun's that it has been suggested that the same artist worked on both.

Horemheb

While Ay had political power, Horemheb had a more direct kind of strength – he was commander-in-chief of the army, and one of his titles was 'Deputy of the King'. He reasserted Egypt's control of some parts of the empire and made sure that tribute continued

to flow in. He built himself a private tomb at Saqqara near Memphis, but succeeded Ay as pharaoh and built a more appropriate one in the Valley of the Kings. It's been suggested that his accession may not have been entirely smooth – his links with the royal family appear to have been administrative rather than based on family relationships – and he certainly asserted his legitimacy and authority quite markedly once he became ruler. One of Ay's relatives, Nakhtmin, gave five shabti figures to Tutankhamun's tomb; he was another army officer. A statue of this man has been found which dates to Ay's reign, and on it Nakhtmin is described as 'King's son'. This may have been a figurative description, but whether it was or not, he disappears. Maya also gave figures to the tomb, and they record his titles. He was the 'Overseer of Works in the Place of Eternity' – the royal cemetery – and of the Treasury. Maya seems to have been responsible for preparing Tutankhamun's tomb after his death, and also for restoring it after the visit by the robbers. Maya lived through several reigns and built his own tomb at Saqqara, where it has recently been rediscovered. The gifts of shabti figures from both Maya and Nakhtmin indicates that they were close to the king.

There are a few others whose names are known but who, apart from that, remain shadowy. Two viziers are recorded,

Usermont and Pentu, and the viceroy of Kush during Tutankhamun's reign was Amenhotep-Huy, who had a tomb at Thebes. His (probable) wife, Taemwadjsi, is described as 'chief of the harem of Tutankhamun', but that is all that is known of her and, indeed, of the boy king's harem.

Above: The deities Horus and Hathor either side of Horemheb in a painting from Horemheb's tomb in the Valley of the Kings. Horemheb returned Egypt completely to the 'old' religion when he took over as pharaoh following Ay's death, and set about eradicating any traces of Akhenaten, his beliefs and his immediate successors. The commander of Tutankhamun's army, Horemheb may actually have held the same post, or a very similar one, under Akhenaten. His large tomb in the Valley of the Kings was discovered in 1908, but very little remained of the grave goods it had once contained.

Opposite: Ay ruled for four years after Tutankhamun's death, and appears to have been related to the royal family. By performing the 'Opening of the Mouth' ceremony for Tutankhamun he was stressing his right to rule. Almost all images of Ay were destroyed in antiquity, beginning in the reign of Horemheb, probably because of his association with Akhenaten's heretical regime.

Death of a Pharaoh

Tutankhamun died some time in January; he was only about 19 years old. Flowers and fruit left in his tomb have enabled archaeologists to determine what time of year he died – the period of embalming was generally a standard 70 days – but there has been endless speculation about how. There have been many theories, from the mundane to the melodramatic, and his body has been examined several times in search of an answer. However,

there is still no evidence from his mummy which clarifies matters, though some things can be ruled out.

Unfortunately the unguents which had been poured over Tutankhamun's body had been applied so lavishly that 'some kind of slow spontaneous combustion' had occurred inside the coffin. Both the wrappings and the body had been almost destroyed and very little remained other than bones and ashes, in contrast to many royal mummies. The body had also been damaged in the process of extracting it from the remains of solidified resins and bandages, and while removing the burial jewellery. An autopsy was carried out by Douglas Derry in November 1925. The body was so fragile that this was done on site, and Derry was unable to reach any conclusion about the cause of death. It was re-examined in 1968, 1978 and, most recently, in 2005.

The 1968 X-rays showed what seemed to be a denser spot at the back of the skull, which could be interpreted as a chronic subdural haematoma – the result of a blow, accidental or deliberate. Speculation that Tutankhamun had been murdered when he began to assert his own authority, probably by his advisor Ay, had long been rife and this was seen as confirmation. A small piece of bone was also discovered in the skull cavity, and again this was linked with a head injury. The X-rays did discount one suggestion – tuberculosis.

Evidence from the CAT Scan

The 2005 re-examination took the form of a CAT scan. A CAT scanner makes a series of X-ray slices which are assembled on computer to give an image far superior to a conventional X-ray, and CAT scans have been performed on several mummies. Tutankhamun's revealed no sign of any blow to the head and, as the multinational researchers stated emphatically and unanimously, no other sign of foul play whatsoever. They noted the presence of two, not one, fragments of bone inside the skull, and agreed that they would have become stuck in the embalming material which was introduced into the skull cavity had they been there before mummification; Tutankhamun's brain was removed by the embalmers. These pieces were therefore either broken during the mummification process or when Carter and his team were working on the body.

The multinational scientists were divided, however, on one possibly significant factor. Tutankhamun's left leg was fractured and there was no sign of healing. Some of the researchers believed that this break was caused as Carter's team struggled to remove the king's body from his coffin, and that it did not occur in life; there was no evidence for a haemorrhage or haematoma. The others think that it did happen when Tutankhamun was alive and that the king had an accident in which he broke his leg badly. This would have left an open wound, they suggest, and infection could easily have set in – but they also accept that this damage, too, might have been caused by the embalmers.

So there is still no definite cause of death for the young pharaoh, though obvious murder seems to have been ruled out. It is worth considering that not only was it much more common for young people to die then than it is today, but there were also a lot of deaths among younger members of the royal family. Tutankhamun was well nourished and well cared for, as his CAT scan revealed, but it did not protect him from an early death.

However Tutankhamun died, there was evidently some confusion; nobody can have been expecting his reign to end so abruptly. He may well have planned an impressive tomb in the Valley of the Kings – Tomb 23 in the West Valley may have been intended for him – but there was no time to finish anything. Instead

he was interred in a small tomb, typical of those used for high-ranking but private individuals and hastily adapted for royal use; it could have been intended for his principal advisor Ay. The work was probably directed by Maya, who oversaw construction in the royal valley and donated objects for Tutankhamun's burial.

Tutankhamun was childless. Some of the saddest remains from his tomb are those of two premature children, still-born at about five and seven months' gestation. There are signs that the older of the two had spina bifida and Sprengel's deformity, an inherited condition. Ay became the next ruler, performing the 'Opening of the Mouth' ceremony for Tutankhamun's body as recorded in the wall paintings from the tomb, which was one of the ways a new king stressed his right to rule and legitimised his position. He is likely to have made the formal announcement of the king's death, and the process of preparing the tomb and collecting the possessions which Tutankhamun would need in the Afterlife would begin. The body was to remain with the embalmers for 70 days, so his officials would not have had long; many of the items they collected had originally been prepared for other royal burials but were never used. They were adapted for Tutankhamun by changing the names inscribed or written on them, and it is sometimes possible to work out for whom they were originally intended – often Akhenaten.

Right: The 2005 CAT scan of Tutankhamun's body revealed no evidence of deliberate violence, but it did show up a fractured left leg. Howard Carter's team had noticed that the left kneecap was loose (it's now completely separated) which might suggest further damage to that leg. Some of the experts involved believe that this happened in life, and may have caused the king's death when it became infected, though it could have been caused by the embalmers. The others think it happened during Carter's investigations.

Opposite: An elaborately carved calcite perfume jar from the outermost shrine of Tutankhamun's Burial Chamber.

Above: A gold plaque from Tutankhamun's burial showing the king in a chariot. It has been suggested that the injury to his left leg may have been caused by a chariot accident shortly before his death – if it occurred in life.

Making a Tomb in the Royal Valley

Tutankhamun, though undoubtedly now the Valley of the Kings' most well-known inhabitant, was actually one of many. To date there are some 80 tombs and pits in the valley, and not all are of kings; some favoured commoners, such as Tutankhamun's great-grandparents Yuya and Thuya, were permitted to have tombs there as well.

The task of selecting a suitable site would probably have begun early in a king's reign, and there is some evidence that work could even begin on the heir's tomb before the king himself had died. Digging a tomb was a long process and most of the royal tombs are unfinished to some extent. An early death, like that of Tutankhamun, could cause problems. Once the king had died there were only about 70 days – the length of time allowed for mummification – to finish work, whether that was

quarrying, plastering or painting a tomb, so a sudden death could be equally problematic.

During most of the 18th Dynasty tombs were excavated in the cliffs around the valley, sometimes with their entrances in natural clefts. Tutankhamun's grandfather, Amenhotep III, was the first whose tomb entrance was lower down. As with most things in Ancient Egypt, the symbolism of a particular site would have been important. There were probably maps, particularly as time went on and the valley filled up, but none have yet been found; they would have been needed to stop a new tomb from being quarried into the path of an older one. There were some near misses.

The site was chosen and approved – and probably visited – by the king, and work could begin once foundation ceremonies had been completed. Surface debris and sand would be removed and teams of workmen could then quarry into the limestone which lay below. The first door was generally created as soon as the men were deep enough into the limestone to allow them to cut a door of sufficient height with a good lintel above it. Then began the really skilled part.

Working underground

Above ground, laying out a monument was comparatively easy. Below the surface it was a different story; mapping a tomb out in advance was impossible but it still had to be straight, with parts that were level, and ran true. The limestone was relatively easy to quarry, but there were flint nodules which slowed things down – particularly given that the only tools were made from copper, bronze, stone or wood. Metal chisels would be struck with wooden mallets, and spikes and heavy pounding tools were also used. Once the workers were out of daylight, they worked by the light of oil lamps, twisted linen wicks forming oil 'candles'. The quarrymen went first, their debris being removed in wicker baskets or leather containers, and were closely followed by stoneworkers who smoothed and prepared all the surfaces of the corridors and chambers. After them came the plasterers, patching damaged or uneven surfaces and then applying smooth plaster on top. The final layer, of fine gypsum plaster, readied the walls for the painters.

There are some existing records of how the work was done, and it seems that workers were divided into two shifts, morning and afternoon, with a break around noon. Only a few people could have worked at the cutting end of a tomb, especially when narrow corridors were being created. As work progressed the number of people required would have varied, but tombs under construction must often have been crowded, with labourers removing rubble, and stonemasons, plasterers and painters working away in various places.

Progress reports were made – some exist and occasionally record construction problems – and the work would be inspected regularly. If time permitted, original plans could be extended; generally work was cut short by the king's death. And then the new king would start the process once again, in another place, if his tomb had not already been started during the reign of his predecessor.

Right: The entrance to the tomb of Amenhotep II in the Valley of the Kings. The rough, creviced walls provided some camouflage for the royal tombs, but not enough. Like the others, this one was robbed in antiquity.

Opposite: Construction workers were organised into teams. Here one small team is shown dragging a block of stone, possibly one intended for the construction of a mortuary temple.

Exploring Tutankhamun's Tomb

When Howard Carter peered through the small opening he had made in a sealed door, the 'wonderful things' he saw were just the start...

The Antechamber

When Howard Carter and his companions entered the first room of Tutankhamun's tomb, which became known as the Antechamber, their initial impression was of an extraordinary variety of objects. The introduction of electric light did nothing to diminish this aspect of semi-organised chaos. By now, Carter had realised that the tomb had been disturbed twice by robbers after its original closure following the king's burial, and the Antechamber looked as though many of the objects in it had only been put back in a vague semblance of order before the last resealing. A path was cleared in the middle of the room, running between the objects to the right and left; it is not clear to what extent this was enlarged by Carter and his team.

Opposite the entrance from the corridor stood three ritual couches of gilded wood, with sides in the form of elongated animals. These had been lined up against the wall, nose to tail

with a space at each end, and their strangeness disconcerted Carter when he first picked them out in the torchlight. They are tall, between 1.34 and 1.53 metres in height, and vary in length between 1.8 and 2.37 metres. The animals have features picked out in inlay and the middle one, representing a cow goddess, has inlaid trefoils all over the surface to give the impression of hide. The heads of the left-hand one, which was in the form of the part-hippopotamus, part lioness, part-crocodile goddess Ammut, have teeth made of ivory.

Items were positioned beneath and on top of the couches, especially the central and right-hand ones; an access hole low in the wall behind the third led to another room. In front of them was a line of objects, among which were boxes and a folding stool made of ebony partly covered with inlay and gold foil, giving the impression of animal skin. Some of the things found under and on top of the couches had not been put back very tidily, but among them the excavators could see the now-famous golden throne. A small golden shrine was also found behind the third couch; it may have been moved from underneath it by Carter and Carnarvon when they investigated the opening and gained access to the Annexe.

Opposite the couches, to the left of the entrance, was what Carter described as 'a confused mass of chariots, glistening with gold and inlay.' There were four chariots here, dismantled but complete, and each one had had its axle sawn through so that it would fit into the tomb through the entrance corridor. They had been disturbed by the robbers and were in a precarious heap which proved difficult to disentangle.

To the right of the entrance, against the right-hand or northern wall, stood a pair of life-size statues, protecting what looked like another plastered and sealed doorway. Before them was a magnificent painted box, every part decorated with beautifully detailed scenes, which was moved by Carter and Carnarvon to help obscure their early investigation of the

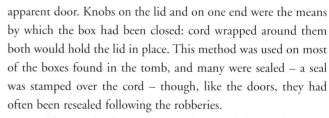

apparent door. Knobs on the lid and on one end were the means by which the box had been closed: cord wrapped around them both would hold the lid in place. This method was used on most of the boxes found in the tomb, and many were sealed – a seal was stamped over the cord – though, like the doors, they had often been resealed following the robberies.

Close to this box were some desiccated funeral bouquets and the two guardian statues, which were still draped in fragments of linen shawls. The figures are made of painted and gilded wood and are not a matching pair, though they are very similar: they have different headdresses, for one thing, and the inscriptions on one of them show that it represents the ka of the king. Clearing the Antechamber began in late December and took until 16 February, by which time all that remained were the guardian statues, still keeping watch. They were left until the next season.

Above: Tutankhamun's tomb in plan, showing the steps, entrance corridor and the four chambers. The Burial Chamber was almost entirely filled by the series of shrines built around the king's sarcophagus.

Left: The golden shrine, one of the most delicate items from the tomb. The whole shrine is only 50 cm high, and is covered with embossed and chased scenes, 18 of which depict the king and queen in informal, intimate settings which may have had a symbolic significance.

Opposite: Even though some items may have been moved between discovery and photography, the early photographs still convey the impression of semi-controlled chaos that greeted Howard Carter and Lord Carnarvon.

The Annexe

If the Antechamber had presented a confused picture to the excavators, the Annexe was infinitely worse, and it was the last chamber to be cleared. It was entered by a plastered doorway under the southernmost of the three ritual couches in the Antechamber, and this had been breached by the robbers. Unlike those in the other doors, though, the hole the thieves made here had not been repaired by the restoration party.

A scene of chaos

The floor of the Annexe was over a metre lower than the level of the Antechamber, and the chaos inside looked complete. Carter said it defied description, and added that 'in the Antechamber there had been some sort of an attempt to tidy up after the plunderers' visit, but here everything was in confusion, just as they had left it'. Actually, much of the confusion was probably due to the activities of the people who reinstated the tomb; they seem to have thrown anything into the Annexe that could not be housed easily elsewhere.

Originally the room may have been intended as a store for most of the oil, unguents, wine and food included in the tomb, something which became apparent as the Annexe was carefully and laboriously cleared. The clutter was piled throughout the chamber, reaching a height of 1.8 metres in some places. Beneath a mass of furniture and miscellaneous objects were many containers – nearly 40 pottery wine jars, alabaster jars holding precious unguents or oils and 116 baskets of fruit… and it looked as though the Annexe had been the main store for the provisions Tutankhamun would need in the Afterlife. A relatively small room, the Annexe does not appear to have been large enough, and meat stored in containers underneath one of the Antechamber couches may have been an 'overflow'. However, some furniture and other items appear to have been included in the Annexe originally, so there may have been a level of disorganisation in filling the tomb in the first place, as well as in its restoration. For instance, Tutankhamun was accompanied into the Afterlife by some 400 shabti figures – who would do any menial work in his place – and some 236 of them were found in the Annexe. A more suitable place would have been the Antechamber or the Treasury.

Among the array of objects found in the Annexe were pieces of furniture, both large – like a day bed; four beds were

found there – and small. One remarkable discovery was a travelling bed. This is hinged so that it would fold into a Z shape for convenience; the extra legs needed to prevent the bed from collapsing when open (and in use) are also hinged, so they would fold inwards too.

Above: A ceremonial shield from Tutankhamun's tomb depicts the king as a sphinx trampling his enemies.

EXPLORING TUTANKHAMUN'S TOMB

A weapon store

Many of the king's weapons had been stored in the Annexe. There was a bow box – another was found in the Treasury – and 17 bows, 295 arrows and 4 inner-arm braces. Most of these were in the bow box, and they may all have been, originally. Tutankhamun's bows, around 30 of which were found, ranged in size from ones suitable for a child to those for an adult; two swords were found, one of which was also child-sized. There were other things: two fragmentary slings; a couple of 'snake' batons, throwing sticks used in hunting wildfowl, depicted in some tombs; eight shields. One of the boxes found in the Annexe contained a close-fitting leather cuirass, which Carter described as being 'like a bodice without sleeves'.

Some of the material from the Annexe appeared to have been ceremonial, such as the openwork shields or the elaborately decorated bows which would have been impractical in use; other things, like one of the beds, had evidently been used. Investigating and moving the delicately balanced mass of miscellaneous objects required skill and inventiveness from Carter and his team.

Right: Many of the shabti which would accompany Tutankhamun into the Afterlife were found in the Annexe. The shabti figures would be animated in the Afterlife and could perform the menial duties allocated to the king in his place.

Below: Several beds and headrests – supports for the head while lying down, popular in Egypt from the Old Kingdom to the end of the New – were found in the Annexe. This ivory headrest is in the form of Shu, the god of the air; it was found in a cabinet with three others. The kneeling figure of the god supports the top of the headrest, equivalent to him supporting the heavens; the lions at the base represent the eastern and western horizons.

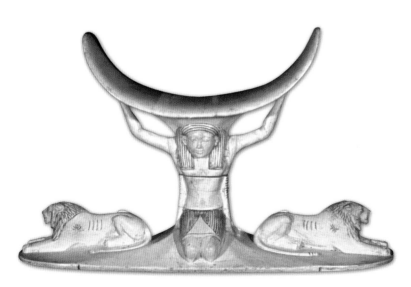

The Burial Chamber

The door between the two guardian statues in the Antechamber was officially opened on 17 February 1923, though it – and the rooms which lay behind it – had been investigated briefly earlier. By this time the Antechamber had been emptied of all its treasures except for the two life-size figures of the king.

Howard Carter eventually made a hole at the top of the plaster which was wide enough to take a torch. What met his gaze was, he records, 'an astonishing sight… for there, within a yard of the doorway, and stretching as far as one could see and blocking the entrance to the chamber, stood what to all appearances was a solid wall of gold…'. This was the outermost of a series of shrines, but there was also an ominous sign. Parts of two broad collars were found on the threshold, lying where they had been dropped by the robbers.

Between the outer shrine and the Burial Chamber walls were many ritual objects, such as 11 magical oars, and another poignant funeral bouquet. These were documented and cleared, and investigations continued. The doors of the shrine, which were at the eastern end, were not sealed; another unsettling indication that the thieves might have penetrated the core of the tomb. These were unbolted and opened, which revealed a linen pall decorated with gilt-bronze daisies and supported on a wooden framework. Below this was another shrine – and this time with its necropolis seal, the jackal and nine captives, intact. Two calcite perfume jars stood in front of the doors, and there were also other items; again they were moved and the doors opened. Then two more shrines were discovered, nested inside. Nothing was found between shrines two and three, but there were bows and two magnificent fans between shrines three and four – and inside the fourth shrine lay the calcite sarcophagus of the king.

The space in the chamber was restricted which made it awkward for the excavators, but it had also been difficult at the time of the king's burial. The shrines had been brought into the chamber in sections, placed in order against the walls and then carefully assembled; more than 150 marks were found, designed to show the correct placing and construction of the separate pieces. Despite this, there had been problems as the sarcophagus was slightly out of true and the innermost shrine had to be adjusted. The third shrine had also needed this attention, but here the necessary amendment had been made by thumping it with a hammer.

Right: Demolishing the door to the Burial Chamber in February 1923. The opening was filled with the brilliant gold and blue of the largest shrine, so close that it almost appeared to block the entrance.

Opposite above: Relief of Nephthys extending her wings to protect the sarcophagus of Tutankhamun.

The sarcophagus

Tutankhamun's huge carved sarcophagus was made from a single block of yellow quartzite with a red granite lid, though it had been painted to match the rest. This could have been an emergency measure, a different lid used because the correct one was not ready in time. It had certainly been problematic, too: it had cracked across the middle, the crack had been filled with gypsum and touched up to blend in with the colour of the lid. The damage could have been the result of an accident when hurrying to install it, but however it had happened, it certainly made the task of lifting the lid some 3250 years later exceptionally difficult.

On 12 February 1924, using a careful pulley system, the lid was gradually lifted up into the air. This revealed Tutankhamun's still-shrouded coffin. The sheets of linen were gently rolled back, bringing a magnificent and enormous golden coffin into view for the first time since the king's burial. Nothing like it had been seen before and its huge size suggested that, like the nested shrines, more coffins might be found inside. But the research and conservation needs of the material already excavated from the tomb meant that further investigation would have to wait.

Right: Howard Carter, together with two members of the excavation team, is looking through the open doors of the golden shrines towards Tutankhamun's sarcophagus; one of the bolts which held the doors closed can be seen clearly. The shrines should ideally have been assembled so that the doors opened to the west, but in the cramped conditions of the Burial Chamber they were constructed the other way round.

The Treasury

There was an door at the eastern end of the Burial Chamber which had never been blocked. It opened into another room which was smaller than the others but full of astonishing objects, many apparently of religious significance. Even at first glance it was possible for the excavators to tell that this particular room held some of the most precious of the goods which had been assembled for the king's Afterlife, and it was accordingly called the Treasury.

At the front of the room and facing the shrines of the Burial Chamber was a figure of Anubis, the god of embalming, in his jackal form. It was swathed in cloth and sat on a shrine mounted on a portable sled which still had its carrying poles; they stuck out into the opening. Another of the glories of Egyptian art, the elegant and watchful Anubis figure was made from wood covered in black resin and the eyes were inlaid with calcite and obsidian; the nails were solid silver. Inside the gilded wooden shrine on which it sat were found a strange assortment of objects, such as four faience models of bovine forelegs, which presumably had a religious significance. Between the jackal's forepaws was an ivory palette inscribed with the name of Tutankhamun's oldest half-sister Meritaten, and the linen shawl it wore was covered by a linen shirt inscribed with a note dating it to the seventh year of Akhenaten's reign.

The gilded shrine

There were numerous boxes and cabinets in the Treasury, some of which had very obviously been disturbed and then refilled – but the disturbance had been selective; the robbers seem to have known exactly where to look. There were also many models of funerary boats, some very beautiful, but the back of the room was dominated by a large gilded shrine which almost touched the ceiling. Carter described it as 'the most beautiful monument that I have ever seen' and said that it made him 'gasp with wonder and admiration'. His opinion was shared by other members of his team: 'It was so wonderful we came out dazzled,' wrote Arthur Mace, who later collaborated with Carter on the first volume of his book about the discovery. This was Tutankhamun's canopic shrine, which was created to shelter his embalmed internal organs.

The gilded wooden shrine is nearly 2 metres high, 1.53 metres long and 1.22 metres wide, and later investigation showed that it was another multi-layered construction. The inner layers are equally beautiful, but at the time of discovery it was the golden exterior that stunned all who saw it. The shrine is topped by a frieze of inlaid coloured uraei – the rearing cobra familiar from royal headdresses – bearing solar discs on their heads, which is repeated a little lower down. It has posts at each corner, and between them on each side stands an elegant figure of a goddess, also made from gilded wood. The four goddesses – Isis, Nephthys, Neith and Selkis – face inwards, their heads turned slightly, with their arms outstretched protectively. They are unique in Egyptian art and conform to the standard grid for representing the human figure used at Amarna.

It was impossible for Carter and his team to clear the Treasury immediately; the vast amount of material already recovered from the tomb needed to be documented, conserved and transported. The opening was blocked by wooden boards while work continued elsewhere, and clearing finally began in October 1926. Among other things, an undecorated box was found which contained two small coffins; its seal had been broken in antiquity. Within each of these coffins was a second, and inside each of those was a small mummified body of a premature baby, one of maybe five months' gestation, the other a little older at possibly seven months. It is highly likely that these are Tutankhamun's children.

Opposite: The canopic shrine from the Treasury showing one of the four protecting goddesses; this is Selkis. The multi-layered shrine, about 2 metres high, held the king's mummified internal organs.

Deir el-Medina

Deir el-Medina was a village on the west side of the Nile, expressly designed to house the craftsmen who built the royal tombs in the Valley of the Kings. Thanks to systematic, careful excavation and research throughout much of the 20th century, more is known about its inhabitants than is known about the great kings whose tombs the villagers created. Many, if not all, of the people were literate and often small pieces of limestone or broken pot were used for writing. Because of this much valuable written evidence of everyday life has been retrieved, and it is possible to establish many details which would otherwise have remained either unknown or hazy.

The origins of the village

The village was founded at the beginning of the 18th Dynasty, probably by Amenhotep I, and was abandoned at the end of the 20th Dynasty after nearly 500 years of occupation. Its purpose was to house people working on the royal tombs, and when kings began to be buried elsewhere it had no reason to exist. A similar village existed at Amarna during Akhenaten's reign.

Deir el-Medina was situated about 3 km away from the valley of the Nile. The houses were made of stone and mudbrick, and generally had four or five rooms. Windows were placed high in the walls, and a staircase led up to the roof. Everyone who was appointed to the workforce of the royal burial ground received one of these houses, and a tomb nearby, as well as a hut in the Valley of the Kings and other things like domestic animals, and maybe a storeroom. The house belonged to the king, however, and could not be passed on to any heirs or divided up. If they wished, people could build their own houses on nearby land which didn't belong to Deir el-Medina, but had to do so in their own time.

Most of the inhabitants of Deir el-Medina were skilled artisans – stonemasons, plasterers, painters, carvers, draughtsmen – and their families also lived in the village. Nearby, and not seen as being part of the Deir el-Medina community, was a settlement scattered outside the village walls. This belonged to the semedet, basic labourers who would not have been directly involved in creating a royal tomb, except as water-carriers or removers of rubble and debris. They were essentially unskilled.

The organisation of the workforce

The skilled craftsmen's time was divided between the village and the Valley of the Kings, where they often stayed in an encampment on the ridge above the Valley. They worked eight days and then had two days off as a sort of 'weekend', when they would return to Deir el-Medina. They also returned for holidays and for various other reasons, some of which are recorded in the scribes' diaries: temple duties, births, deaths, illness, snakebites or even having to take an ailing donkey to the equivalent of the vet. There are records of one absentee having had a fight with his wife, and of another being so hungover following a drinking session with his friend Khons that he was also unable to work.

A lot is known about the way the 'Servants in the Place of Truth', as the community was known, were organised. People were grouped along naval lines; oarsmen in naval ships were divided into 'left' and 'right' sides, and the skilled workers in the Valley of the Kings were organised into left and right teams as well. They were even known as 'The Ship's Crew'. It has been suggested that this division may have reflected the fact that the actual work in a tomb was divided into right- and left-hand sides. Young men seem to have generally taken over their fathers' positions and specialisations, though there are some exceptions, and new members of the community could be appointed by the vizier, acting on information from one of the foremen and one of the scribes. The eldest son would usually be the one who succeeded his parent; others might join the comparatively unskilled semedet community or leave completely. One foreman, Neferhotep, had five sons. The oldest also became a foreman; the second son went into the army and became an officer-scribe; the third son was an officer in the Ramesseum; the occupation of the fourth was not recorded and the fifth was still a boy when this information was written down.

Opposite: The artisans' village of Deir el-Medina has provided an astonishing range of information about the way its inhabitants spent their time, largely due to the number of written records which have been retrieved. The people who lived there called their village 'Pa-demi', the town, and their names were often inscribed on the lintels of their houses, so it is sometimes possible to know who lived where.

Below: The Deir el-Medina tomb of Sennedjem is one of the most beautifully painted tombs in all of Egypt. The large painting on the end wall of his burial chamber show him and his wife Iynefert working in the fields of the Afterworld. Everything is in abundance; crops grow tall and the date palms are laden with fruit.

to-day matters such as the distribution of tools. There were others in official positions, such as the 'Guardians of the Tomb'. These men looked after the stores, issuing new tools – under the supervision of the scribes – and arranging for worn or broken ones to be repaired. They also issued such things as lighting materials and artists' pigments. The tools, especially the copper ones, were extremely valuable.

Life in Deir el-Medina

Deir el-Medina was walled, and the people within it were not exactly free; they were tied to their place of work, to the vizier and ultimately to the pharaoh himself. They were not permitted to leave their jobs unless seconded elsewhere, though they could be demoted to the ranks of the semedet. They could move about freely, however, even though they were secluded in their particular village. There is no evidence that they were watched closely though that might have seemed advisable – after all, these people knew the location of the royal tombs. The walls appear to have been there to protect the village from thieves, to keep people out rather than in.

There were two foremen, one for each 'side' – they were called 'Great Ones of the Crew', pushing the nautical analogy further. These men were never outsiders, and they were the link between the members of the crew and their superiors, even with the vizier. Each team also had a 'deputy', and these men seem to have been ordinary craftsmen rather than children of deputies or foremen. They were spokesmen for the crew but also did things like handing out rations and deputising for the foremen. Scribes were important; they recorded the work taking place, supplies received and issued, any absences, payments and any other day-

Inscriptions in the tombs, together with the documents recovered, show that Deir el-Medina was somewhat cosmopolitan, perhaps as a result of the best craftsmen in the kingdom being concentrated in one place: over 30 foreign names have been found. It was also a rather religious community, with many small temples, shrines and the votive stones which honour the ancestors of the people working there. For most of the time, the majority of the people living in the village would have been women and children; the men would have been away in the Valley. Their wives had many responsibilities and there is one

clear case of a foreman's wife actually paying out wages when her husband was away. Many of them also had religious duties.

On days off the inhabitants could undertake private work; some of them evidently did a good trade in funerary equipment. Anything made in their own time, using their own tools and materials, became their personal property which they were free to sell. They would also have worked on their own tombs and those of their colleagues, and some of the tombs of Deir el-Medina are among the most beautiful in Egypt – their makers were, after all, the best. Some of the craftsmen were minor priests in their spare time.

Reading was a popular activity (so, it appears, was adultery), and court cases were also entertaining. The village conducted its own legal affairs; the judges were the foremen, deputies, a scribe and some of the craftsmen. Major crimes fell under the jurisdiction of the vizier's court over the river in Thebes, but this local court could deal with minor crimes and civil actions. Most of the cases were relatively trivial, often concerning disputes over payment, and could take years to resolve; as the villagers conducted their own cases and there were

no expensive fees for outsiders, they could take their time. One, over non-payment for some clothing and a container of fat, took 11 years to resolve. In keeping with its remit, the court could only impose minor penalties, generally the return of goods concerned in any property disputes. The court officials had one other duty, however – they had to inspect the tombs in the Valley.

As time went on and Deir el-Medina became more impoverished, some of the inhabitants appear to have turned to a more serious crime: tomb robbing.

Opposite above: Iynefert, Sennedjem's wife, dressed in her best clothes, following her husband and working in the fields of the Afterlife.

Opposite below: Sennedjem and his wife ploughing the fields of the Afterworld. They would not have expected to do this themselves, however; they would have been provided with shabti figures who would undertake such work in their place.

Above: Sennedjem and his wife seated before a priest wearing a leopard skin.

Working to Clear the Tomb

Howard Carter was, in many ways, the best person to have found a tomb like Tutankhamun's. Had it been discovered a decade earlier, or by someone like Theodore Davis, much less trouble would have been taken and irretrievable damage would have been done to one of the most astonishing discoveries ever made. Carter, however, fully appreciated the archaeological significance of what he had found, and one of his first tasks was to put together a team of experts to investigate all aspects of the tomb and help preserve its treasures. They included Alfred Lucas, a chemist who worked on the conservation and analysis of the materials found in the tomb, and who seems to have been the first ever resident chemist on an archaeological site; Percy Newberry who worked on the botanical remains and Alan Gardiner, the foremost expert on Egyptian scripts, who analysed and translated the written material. In the end, clearing the tomb and transporting the finds took almost ten years. Nearby tombs were used as conservation labs, temporary stores or photographic studios.

There were many early problems, mostly political, but the clearance of the tomb generally proceeded methodically and, though some damage was done during a hiatus in which Carter left the site, much was achieved. A routine was quickly established for both removing and processing items. Simply moving them was difficult as altering the position of one object would often endanger others, especially in the more crowded and confused areas of the Antechamber and Annexe. Elaborate systems of supports, props and pulleys were constructed to keep things safe while others were shifted. The situation was worst in the Annexe; here excavators had to be suspended above the piles of artefacts on ropes until they had cleared enough space to enable them to stand. And, of course, the objects they were removing were well over 3000 years old, priceless and very fragile.

Some things had evidently been brought into the tomb in sections and assembled inside, and getting these out again presented special difficulties. The ritual couches were held

records were made. Conditions were not good; the temperatures were high and there was constant harassment from the press (Lord Carnarvon had done an exclusive deal with the London *Times*) who wanted things to progress much faster; at times from the Egyptian government, and always from a constant stream of important visitors.

The antiquities were carefully protected – wrapping and padding those from the Antechamber alone used 32 bales of calico and over a mile of cotton wadding – and were crated for transport. Getting them from the Valley to the river took 15 hours, using a hand-propelled railway with movable rails, of which there were not enough. Boats carried the treasures northwards to Cairo but a few, such as the gold coffin and the famous mask, were taken there by train under armed guard, and the carriage was shunted straight into the yard of the museum.

together with bronze hooks and staples, and took five people to dismantle. The shrines in the Burial Chamber had also been assembled in situ, and presented special problems. They were exceptionally fragile as well as being in a confined space, but they were gradually separated and the panels were rested against the walls of the tomb. They had to be conserved before being moved further because the wood had shrunk, causing the gilded surface to part in some places. It was two more seasons before they could be moved to Cairo.

Photographs were taken in the tomb; an item was then numbered and photographed again and a brief description was written on a record card. Its position would be plotted on the plans and it could then be taken up to conservation, where full

Opposite: Howard Carter supervising carpenters working in Tutankhamun's tomb.

Above and below: Once the objects from the tomb had been safely conserved they were packed into specially built crates and taken down to the Nile for onward transport to Cairo. In all probability they travelled along the same route that they had taken over 3000 years earlier, but in the opposite direction.

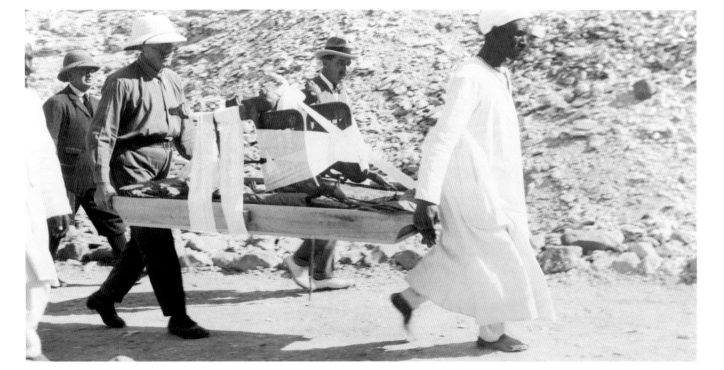

The Paintings from the Tomb

All tomb paintings reflected the Afterlife, but those in royal tombs were rather different; they gave a more detailed and thorough picture of what the spirit of the deceased pharaoh could expect to encounter. Their particular focus changes over time, and in the 18th Dynasty, the time of Tutankhamun, the stress was on the journey of the sun beneath the earth.

The burial chamber

In Tutankhamun's tomb, the decoration is confined to the walls of the Burial Chamber itself. This may be due to his death being unexpected, and a certain amount of improvisation being necessary; had more time been available, things might have been different. The walls of the chamber were covered with a thick layer of smooth plaster, on top of which the paintings were done. Unfortunately they have deteriorated, a process which may have begun shortly after the tomb was closed after completion of the funerary rites. The paintings are spotted by fungal growths, in all probability due to the fact that the tomb was sealed up before the plaster was completely dry. It is thought that the spores were introduced in the materials used, in the plaster itself or in the paint, and that the humidity arising from the damp plaster enabled them to spread after the tomb was shut.

The west wall

The paintings in the tomb were designed to help smooth the king's way into the Afterlife, and would also ensure his

continuing survival in the next world. The focus of the decoration is the west wall, which was behind the head of the sarcophagus. The west was where the underworld lay; it was the place where the sun went at night before being reborn in the east the following morning. This wall is entirely devoted to an extract from 'That Which is in the Underworld', the Amduat, one of the earliest of the Egyptian funerary texts. It details the journey of the sun through the twelve divisions of the underworld, divisions that correspond to the twelve hours of darkness. At the top is a boat holding Khepri, the creator god of the rising sun, represented as a scarab beetle. There are three gods and two goddesses in front of it and below, in three rows of four boxes, are the twelve baboon deities of the twelve hours of night. The sun, and the king, must travel through these before dawn and rebirth, a time of great danger.

All the wall paintings have a yellow background, and are blank – painted white – below a dado, giving them a unity even though the three other walls are very different in design from the western one. Opposite, on the east wall, the mummified body of the king is shown lying in a decorated shrine which rests on a sledge. This is being pulled by twelve men in five groups, who are holding a rope; two have shaven heads and distinctive robes; they are the viziers (or chief ministers) of Upper and Lower Egypt. During Tutankhamun's reign these positions were held at some

point by two men called Usermont and Pentu and they could be the individuals depicted here. All the nobles pulling the sledge are shown as welcoming the dead king to the west in peace.

The north and south walls

The north and south walls show another ceremony directly concerning Tutankhamun's death, and illustrate his welcome into the other world. The north wall, opposite the entrance from the Antechamber, is the most complete and can be divided into three scenes. The first shows Ay, Tutankhamun's successor, first minister and possible relative, performing a ceremony known as the 'Opening of the Mouth'. Ay is wearing the blue crown, a stylised helmet, and the leopard skin of a sem priest, the funerary priest whose part was taken by the heir to the throne at royal

Top: Tutankhamun, now shown as a living king rather than a mummy, is greeted by the goddess Nut in the middle panel of the north wall.

Opposite: Behind the head of the sarcophagus is a painting depicting the twelve hours of the night, the focus of all the decoration. The deceased king, like the sun, must travel through the dangers of the night before being reborn.

funerals. Tutankhamun is shown as Osiris, the god of the dead. Both figures are identified by the hieroglyphics above them. This ceremony was usually performed by a son for his father and emphasised Ay's right to the succession; it prepared the body of the deceased to receive offerings in the Afterlife. In the next scene Tutankhamun, his name written above his figure again, is shown as though he was a living king. He holds a staff in one hand and a mace and ankh symbol in the other, while the accompanying text promises him eternal life. He is being greeted by Nut, the goddess of the sky. In the final scene on the north wall Tutankhamun is shown wearing the nemes headcloth, the striped one familiar from his mask, and is accompanied by his ka or spiritual double, whose ka sign above his head – two upraised arms – encloses the hieroglyphic for one of Tutankhamun's royal names, his Horus name of 'Mighty Bull'. Osiris is welcoming Tutankhamun into the next world with an embrace.

Damage during the excavations

The eastern part of the south wall had evidently been finished once the sarcophagus and shrines were safely installed in the Burial Chamber, and the partition between that and the Antechamber had to be partly demolished to allow removal of the shrines. This meant that the paintings on that wall of the Burial Chamber were inevitably damaged, but Howard Carter recovered as many fragments of the scene as possible and they were documented and photographed. Much still exists, as well. These paintings show Tutankhamun being welcomed into the Afterlife again, this time by Hathor; among her many roles, she was the principal goddess of the west. Anubis, the god of embalming, stands behind Tutankhamun and behind Anubis originally stood a figure of Isis, with three minor deities behind her. This wall is a little different from the others in style, too. It doesn't look as though it was painted by the same person, for one thing: while the rest of the paintings follow the convention of a grid of twenty

squares, as used during the time of Akhenaten, this wall is based on eighteen squares, the more traditional format; the figures appear slimmer. It also seems to have been painted in some haste and was evidently the last one to be done, its decoration completed after the shrines had been assembled in the Burial Chamber.

Generally, excavation and painting of a tomb seems to have happened simultaneously, with the stonecutters working in one place while the plasterers and painters worked in another. In smaller tombs this would have been almost impossible; not only would they have been too cramped, but debris and dust would have damaged the newly painted surfaces. The painting in Tutankhamun's tomb certainly continued on one wall after the

shrines had been constructed around the king's sarcophagus, and there would have been very little room for the artist or artists to work – only about 60 cm separated the outermost shrine from the walls of the chamber.

Above: Tutankhamun, with his ka standing behind him, embraces Osiris, lord of the west.

Opposite: Detail of wall painting from the south wall of Tutankhamun's Burial Chamber. Here he is seen with Anubis and Nephthys.

The King's Coffins

When Howard Carter and his team saw the huge coffin which lay in the sarcophagus at the heart of the golden shrines in Tutankhamun's Burial Chamber, they suspected it might contain others nested inside. It was certainly big enough to be the first of several, at about 2.25 metres long. Initial inspection showed that it rested on a lion-headed gilt bier, similar to those shown in many tomb paintings, which still held despite the enormous weight it had been carrying for over three millennia.

The coffin is beautiful, with feathered decoration referring to the ba, the bird form of the soul, but there had been a problem with fit at the time of the king's burial. The toes of the coffin had been 'adjusted' – shortened with an adze – to permit the sarcophagus lid to close; the bits that had been adzed off were found at the bottom of the sarcophagus. A small wreath of olive leaves and blue flowers bound onto a strip of papyrus had been placed gently around the uraeus on the forehead of the coffin, arranged so that the olive leaves alternately displayed the different colours of their upper and lower surfaces. Further investigation had to wait; there was much to be done with the rest of the tomb and the relationship between the excavating team and the government was problematic.

In October 1925 this coffin was finally opened, using the original silver handles on the lid. Beneath it lay another shrouded coffin, on which were the remains of funeral garlands.

The decision was made at this point to lift the coffins out of the sarcophagus together; it was a difficult job, not least because of the weight, but made subsequent work much easier. Then the second coffin was exposed. It is magnificent, made from wood covered in thick gold foil and inlays of precious materials. Like the outer coffin, it also has a feathered design, but here the feathers are inlaid in red, blue and turquoise; unfortunately some were affected by damp and tended to fall out of position. The face does not look particularly like Tutankhamun, and he may not have been its intended owner. Other items in the tomb had definitely been recycled, and it looks as though that was the case with this coffin as well.

Lifting its lid was less straightforward as it had been held in place with silver nails and had no handles; it was also extremely fragile. Eventually it was removed, and again the shrouded form of a coffin was revealed. The shroud had been made from fine linen and had been placed so that the face of the coffin remained uncovered, as did a delicate collar of beads and leaves. The collar and the linen were removed and the third coffin was finally visible. It was obviously made of solid gold. It was also partly covered in a 'thick pitch-like layer' from the crossed hands to the ankles, the remains of the unguents that had been poured over it and which had now solidified between this third coffin and the base of the second one in which it lay. Removing the black substance was a risky and arduous task, but it was eventually achieved.

The third coffin, made from sheets of heavy gold, weighs 110.4 kg and is 1.88 metres long. The face resembles the first coffin and other portraits of the king and parts are beautifully inlaid, but the inlays which would have formed the eyes have not survived; the rest

has a chased design. Like the second coffin, it also wore a separate necklace – two, in fact – and like the first coffin, it had been fitted with handles. The lid was attached to the base with gold tongues which dropped into slots, the two elements held together by pins. This coffin fitted very snugly inside the second, and the pins had to be carefully removed before the lid could be lifted by its golden handles.

Opposite: Once it had been established that Tutankhamun's shrines and outermost coffin were intact and undamaged, no attempts were made to investigate the coffins further and urgent work – and negotiations – continued elsewhere. The lid of what turned out to be the outermost coffin of three was finally lifted in October 1925, nearly 20 months after the sarcophagus had been opened.

Right: Detail of third coffin of Tutankhamun.

The Mummy of the King

Lifting the lid of the third of Tutankhamun's coffins, the excavating team finally exposed the body of the young king. Again unguents had been extensively used, again they had darkened and solidified over time. The excavators were, however, presented with a beautiful sight despite this because again the feet, together with the head and shoulders, had been avoided. The mummy wore an astonishing and wonderful portrait mask, now one of the most famous treasures in the world.

The mask depicts the young ruler as Osiris, the lord of the Afterlife. It is made from two sheets of gold, joined together by hammering, and is decorated in carnelian, lapis lazuli, turquoise and glass paste. The eyes are made from quartz and obsidian and were given a realistic appearance by a touch of red at the corners; the realism is further enhanced by the natural look of the ears which are not symmetrical. The ears are pierced and the holes were originally covered by discs of gold foil; boys wore earrings during Tutankhamun's time, but men did not.

The mask was not, however, the only thing the mummy wore. A scarab had been hung around its neck, a pair of golden hands had been fastened to the bandages and there were other items, including mummy bands, gold strips binding the shrouded and bandaged corpse. These had not been made for Tutankhamun; some of the original names had been removed and they had been adjusted to fit – parts had been cut out and the remaining strips pieced closer together.

Unwrapping the king

At first it looked as though the mummy might be in good condition, but closer examination quickly showed that the opposite was the case. The outer shroud had been badly affected by the unguents, which had been used in quantity, and both the mummy and its glorious mask were stuck firmly in the coffin. And that was where the first investigation of Tutankhamun's body had to take place in November 1925, in an autopsy conducted by Dr Douglas Derry and Dr Saleh Bey Hamdi.

Because of the state of the mummy, the wrappings were removed in pieces rather than the bandages being unwound. During this process 150 items of ritual jewellery – including necklaces, collars, amulets and two daggers – were discovered, carefully arranged in particular places on the body or in the

Right: Included in the wrappings of Tutankhamun's mummy were two daggers, the finest of all the weapons found in the tomb. One was tucked under a chased belt that encircled the waist, and the other was found in the wrappings of the right thigh. Both were in their scabbards and the one on the waist had a blade of hardened gold. The blade of the one found over the king's thigh, however, was of a much rarer and much more precious material – iron.

Opposite: The golden mask found over the head and shoulders of Tutankhamun's mummy is one of the most famous of ancient artefacts; the quality of the work is exceptionally high and the mask is breathtaking. There is an engraved inscription on the back and shoulders which is intended to protect the mask and the king's head which it covered. It does appear to be a portrait, even if slightly idealised.

bandages. Their purpose was to help the dead king pass safely into the Afterlife. As work continued, the scale of the deterioration caused by the ancient unguents became apparent; the inner wrappings were so badly damaged that any detail of the bandaging itself had been destroyed. Care had been taken, though, and the embalming of Tutankhamun's body had not been rushed or improvised. That much was clear.

After four days' work the team had worked their way upwards to the neck, and in order to free the body from the coffin it had to be dismantled. Now came one of the most potentially difficult tasks – removing the mask from the head and shoulders. These were firmly stuck inside the mask, and Carter was worried that separating them would require the use of 'drastic measures'. Fortunately warmed knives were all that was needed, and it was soon possible to see the face of the young king; his head had been shaved and his ears had indeed been pierced. He had evidently been between 17 and 19 when he died; the most recent research tends towards 19. When alive he would probably have been about 2.5 cm taller than his mummy, which was 1.63 metres tall, just over 5 ft 4 in. This was exactly the height of the two figures who stood in the Antechamber, guarding the doorway into the Burial Chamber.

Art for the Afterlife

Many Egyptian tombs, not just those belonging to members of the royal family, are beautifully decorated with carved reliefs and wall paintings, their colours still bright even today. They are some of the most evocative of Ancient Egyptian remains, with their scenes of everyday life – or everyday life in the Afterlife. The wall paintings were not just decoration; they represented the next world and could even provide a guide for the deceased. The artists illustrated many things, in the context of the Afterlife, from banquets, harvests and hunts to the journey of the spirit after death. They were aspirational, an idealised view of the life the tomb owner would hope to have in the next world, so people are shown in their best clothes, even when depicted ploughing the fields. And, of course, these paintings were never supposed to be seen by living eyes once the tomb had been sealed.

The artist at work

In smaller tombs, and in larger ones when close to the entrance, artists could work by reflected sunlight; most of the time, however, oil lamps would have been used. Generally, the painters would have laid out a grid on the plastered wall with measuring rods and string covered in paint which was held against the surface. The original design would also have been done on a grid, but a much smaller one, and once the large grid was marked on the wall the painter would carefully transfer the design, probably copying it one square at a time. The outlines were completed in red paint, then corrected and a final outline done in black. Any errors in the text would be corrected at this point, too.

Artistic conventions

Conventions had to be followed in the design. Important people were drawn much larger than children, servants or those bringing them offerings, and the human figure was depicted in a stylised way. It was shown as though viewed simultaneously from several angles, with the head, arms and legs in profile; the shoulders and eyes as though seen from the front, and with the body oddly twisted from a frontal view at the shoulders to a sideways view

Above: Part of the painted ceiling from Seti I's tomb in the Valley of the Kings. It shows a map of the night sky, with the figures of the Egyptian zodiac. This was the first tomb to have all its passages and chambers decorated, and the quality is outstanding.

lower down. There was no attempt at perspective, and people or objects which were in front of other things would be shown as overlapping them. Inaccuracies could easily creep in – in one Theban tomb a group of women mourn the high official Ramose; there are five heads but only four bodies.

The use of colour

There were also conventions in the use of colour. Colours were relatively limited; throughout the Valley of the Kings, for example, only six were used – red, black, white, yellow, green and blue – but they were sometimes mixed together. A pale yellow was used for female skin tones, a brownish red for male skin; yellow or blue-green were used for the bodies of the gods and yellow also symbolised eternity; blue was used for the sky, but also for the gods' hair. Skin colour was also used to define nationality; people from Asia were shown as being a rather pasty white, while Nubians, for example, were shown as having very dark skin. Ceilings were sometimes painted in a deep blue to represent the night sky, and were sparkled with golden yellow stars.

The colours were generally mineral pigments, with egg white and gum arabic added to bind them together, and brushes were made out of reed stems, with one end frayed by chewing. Mineral pigments hold their colour much better than vegetable-derived ones, and this is one of the reason why so much of the art is so glowing today.

The art often seems so formal that it is difficult to think of the artists having much scope for the imagination. But they were just as creative as artists the world over; though most of the time they worked within strict rules and conventions the work they produced is beautiful and often moving. They let their hair down, too, producing cartoons and sketches on pottery shards or scraps of limestone. These show all sorts of things – lively dancers, an unshaven stonemason (which must be a portrait), a cat serving a duck to a mouse sitting on a stool – and give quite another view of Ancient Egyptian artists.

Above: A representation of Annubis, the jackal-headed god, from the tomb of Amon-hir-Khopshef.

Left: Not all wall painting was grand, imposing and royal; some, such as this one of a harvest offering, was much more informal.

Robbers in the Tomb

Tutankhamun's was the seventh royal burial in the Valley of the Kings. The architect of the first tomb, that of Tuthmosis I, recorded on the walls of his own: 'I built the tomb of my master, no one seeing, no one hearing.' It was hoped that the landscape of the valley, together with its distance from settlements, would obscure the location of the royal tombs, but building them with 'no one seeing, no one hearing' was impossible. All the tombs were robbed in antiquity, including Tutankhamun's. There are even contemporary documents from later in the New Kingdom describing thefts which had taken place and detailing interrogations and punishments.

Gold was not the only temptation. All metal was worth retrieving; glass was particularly precious during the 18th Dynasty; wood and ivory are specified in the documents; linen often vanished. So did fresh perfume and cosmetics, stolen if the tomb was entered shortly after burial. There were periodic inspections of the Valley, generally during the cooler seasons and

in unsettled times when the threat of depredation was strongest, and many of the robberies were probably discovered during these checks. Any thieves who were caught faced torture – for both confessions and more information, as did friends and family – and were likely to be executed by being impaled on a stake.

Robbers had entered Tutankhamun's tomb twice, once very soon after the burial and again probably only a few years later. On both occasions the thefts were discovered – some of the second group may even have been caught in the act – and the tomb restored and resealed by the officials of the royal necropolis. Because of the care taken during the excavation, and because of the notes (or 'dockets') on some items, it is now possible to assess roughly what was taken and what happened.

Initially the entrance corridor was empty, apart from some items which had been stored there: remains from the funeral, left-over material from the king's embalming. These were later removed by the necropolis guards after they discovered the

first robbery and before they filled the corridor with rubble in the hope of preventing others. The items were buried in a nearby pit (now Pit 54), which was found by Theodore Davis. Some other bits and pieces found in the corridor when it was cleared by Carter's team may have been dropped by the thieves; where they can be identified, they seem to have come from the Antechamber, though it is likely that the Annexe was also entered. Metal was removed but so were linen and cosmetics – the fat-based cosmetics used in Ancient Egypt deteriorated quickly and would not have been worth taking had the robbery taken place any later than soon after the funeral.

The second robbery seems to have been more extensive; digging through the now-filled corridor alone would have required time and effort. Once inside, the thieves entered every room and may even have broken the seal on the outermost shrine in the Burial Chamber. They were particularly selective in the Treasury, opening the caskets containing the king's jewels, though they also briefly investigated one of the wooden shrines. They appear to have known exactly where the items that interested them would be, and may have been involved in filling the tomb in the first place. Using the dockets, notes listing original contents, Carter was able to estimate that 60 per cent of the jewellery had been stolen. Some of the thieves may have been interrupted, as a knotted linen scarf full of gold rings had been put into one of the boxes in the Antechamber, doubtless by those restoring the tomb. Most of the stolen jewellery remained missing.

The restoration party worked swiftly – they may have been anxious not to attract too much attention – and restored much of the tomb to a semblance of order. The Annexe was still chaotic and boxes that had been opened were not resealed. The doors, however, were, and the tomb was left for the last time in over 3000 years.

Above: A calcite chalice in the form of a white lotus was one of the first items seen by the excavators – it had been abandoned and lay in the doorway of the Antechamber. The inscription reads: 'Live, your ka, and may you spend millions of years, you lover of Thebes, sitting with your face to the north wind and your eyes beholding happiness.'

Left: This necklace was found in one of the boxes in the Treasury and seems to have been deliberately avoided by the robbers. The main pectoral pendant is of gold inlaid with semi-precious stones and symbolically shows the sun about to rise into the sky.

Opposite: Most of the tombs in the Valley of the Kings had been robbed by the end of the New Kingdom. Tomb robbing proved impossible to prevent, despite the appalling penalties faced by those who were caught – mutilation or execution.

The King's Canopic Shrine

One of the most remarkable finds from the tomb is the large and beautiful shrine which dominated the back of the Treasury and astounded those who saw it. It needed to be dismantled in order to remove it from the tomb – like the shrines around the sarcophagus, it appeared to have been assembled in place – and examining it properly was not possible until the room was emptied during the 1927–8 season. Until then it remained intact and in position, its guardian goddesses still holding out their arms in protection. It was known, however, that this structure was the Canopic shrine – an old term for these, arising from a misunderstanding – which would have contained the king's mummified and embalmed internal organs.

The gilded outer casing had a separate post at each corner supporting a canopy; this gave it an overall height of 1.98 metres and it barely cleared the ceiling. The goddesses Isis, Nephthys, Selkis and Neith are also part of this outer framework, standing slightly away from the walls of the shrine they guard. The framework and the gilded chest were removed, revealing the Canopic chest itself, which had been covered with a folded pall of dark linen. Once this had been taken off the excavators were faced with a carved chest, the main part of which was made from a single block of translucent veined calcite. Details were picked out in dark blue and the same four goddesses were carved on each corner. It stood on a gilded wooden sledge of its own; the whole shrine rested on a much larger one.

The canopic jars

When the lid was removed, four human-headed stoppers could be seen; they were in two pairs and faced each other. Each represented the king – or a king, probably a close family member: some scholars see a resemblance to Tutankhamun while others do not – wearing the striped nemes headcloth. All four are hollowed out below and have a small symbol on them indicating where they belonged; their features are picked out delicately in black and red. Beneath these lids were four deeper hollows which had been drilled into four compartments, and each one contained a small decorated coffin, made of gold but wrapped in linen and anointed with unguents. These small delicate coffins contained the king's wrapped internal organs, and are decorated on both the upper and lower surfaces of the inside, as well as on the exterior.

Left: The calcite chest was inside the golden shrine, and had been covered with a linen shroud. The single block of calcite from which the main part was carved had probably been chosen because of the delicate natural pattern of veins, and the frieze at the bottom is covered in gold leaf. It stands on its own sledge, and the means by which the lid was secured in place can just be seen at the side.

Was the shrine intended for Tutankhamun?

Despite the markers intended to enable the people assembling the shrine get everything in the right position, some mistakes had been made. The freestanding golden figures of Isis and Nephthys were in each other's places and two of the small coffins had also been transposed. It also appears that some elements of the shrine had originally been made for someone other than Tutankhamun, as had some of the other items included in his tomb. The question of whether the stoppers are portraits of the king or not is one possible piece of evidence, but the small coffins provide a more definite one: the parts of the interior inscriptions which give the owner's name have been changed.

Above: Removing the lid of the calcite chest revealed four stoppers in the form of human heads, possible portraits of the king. The cobra and the vulture's head symbols on the foreheads of each one were carved separately and inserted in position.

Right: The four goddesses who protect the Canopic shrine containing Tutankhamun's embalmed internal organs are beautifully sculpted and gilded. Their eyebrows, the outlines of their eyes and their irises are all painted in black; their eyes are white. The naturalistic carving is typical of work produced during the Amarna period, the time of Tutankhamun's predecessor Akhenaten.

Famous Finds

When Howard Carter peered into the first room of Tutankhamun's tomb he reported that he saw 'wonderful things'. Everything the tomb included could be described as wonderful, but some objects stand out.

A small gilded shrine was discovered in the Antechamber, where it still rested on a sledge covered in silver. Its shape copies that of an ancient shrine, and every part is covered with decoration. The whole thing is just over 50 cm tall but there are 18 panels showing scenes of Tutankhamun and Ankhesenamun, and what space remains is covered in inscriptions. There are two doors at the front and Carter's team found the base of a statuette inside, but the rest had gone, probably stolen by the robbers. The intimate informality and relaxed style of the scenes – Ankhesenamun passing an arrow to her husband or anointing his collar, or the couple holding hands – recalls the art of the Amarna period rather than the formality more common at other times.

Another unique and famous find from the Antechamber is the golden throne and, like the small golden shrine, it has all the signs of the Amarna period. Here the symbolism is clear, as the disc of the Aten is shown on the decorated back of the throne above the figures of the king and queen, sending its rays down towards them in benediction. It was probably made during the early years of Tutankhamun's reign, as the royal

Right: The golden throne found in the Antechamber is actually made of wood overlaid with both gold and silver – seen at its best in the queen's robe – and inlaid with semi-precious stones, coloured glass and faience. Six chairs were found in the tomb; this is the most spectacular.

There were over 50 boxes and chests in the tomb, excluding ritual shrines and game boxes, and all of them had been rifled by the robbers. The Antechamber contained the best known, the painted box. It is comparatively small – standing nearly 45 cm high, 43 cm wide and 61 cm long – but every part is covered in multicoloured painted decoration, the most striking panels showing the king in his chariot, either hunting or in battle. Originally it had contained a range of clothing worn by the king as a child, and some was still inside; emptying it took three days. Some items, like a pair of sandals, were in perfect condition, but others were not. A beaded robe disintegrated when it was touched.

Another magnificent chair came to light in the Annexe, where a mass of other furniture was found. The seat is similar to that of a folding stool from the

names appear in their 'old' forms of Tutankhaten and Ankhesenpaaten, and it was evidently altered in other ways after manufacture: both the queen's wig and the headdresses shown have been changed. Grilles originally linked the legs and may have been removed by the thieves. Three millennia later the throne was found under one of the three ritual couches; it had been partly wrapped in black linen.

Antechamber, though the chair is rigid; it is made of ebony and the surface is entirely decorated with inlay. It was probably made during the Amarna period; like the golden throne, there is a prominent solar disc and the king's name is given in both its original form and the amended one of Tutankhamun. This chair had also been wrapped up in black linen.

Above: The detail on the small golden shrine is even more astonishing when its size is considered. Eighteen well-executed panels are present on an object only 50.5 cm tall, 32 cm deep and 26.5 cm wide. It is a work of great skill, and the precise means by which it was made are still not entirely clear.

Right: The beautiful painted box found in the Antechamber had contained some of the king's childhood clothing; some still remained. The decorative detail on the box is very fine; for example, the king can be seen to have tied the reins of his chariot's horses around his waist so that he can use both hands.

Figures from the Tomb

Many human figures were discovered in Tutankhamun's tomb, ranging from the two life-size guardian statues of the king in the Antechamber to the large number of shabtis who would do his work in the Afterworld. There were also other ritual figures, their precise purpose uncertain.

The guardian statues were some of the first things seen by the tomb's discoverers, caught in the light of their torches as they gazed, stunned, around them. The two black and gold figures had been draped in linen shawls, parts of which remained in place. They are made in wood and any uneven parts were filled with plaster before they were finished. The flesh parts are painted in a thick black resin, probably symbolising the earth as these are ka images, stressing the king's rebirth and ultimately indestructible nature. The kilts, headcloths, jewellery, sandals, staffs and other regalia are gilded, and the eyes are made from limestone and obsidian, encircled by gilded bronze. The uraei on the front of the headdresses are also made in bronze. They are portraits of the king, and match his height, confirmed by the study of his mummy. It has been suggested that they may once have contained the king's missing religious texts, hidden in spaces hollowed out on the underside of the kilts.

There were 35 major hardwood figures, most of which were found in the Treasury, generally stored in boxes and wrapped in linen cloths. Two match and are among the most remarkable; they show the king as the god Horus, harpooning a hippopotamus, the symbol of evil. The king is standing on a papyrus raft in the act of hurling a spear, concentrating on his aim. The arms were made separately from the body, and the left hand holds a coil of rolled bronze, a rope which will be used to capture the animal.

Tutankhamun had been provided with over 400 shabti figures who would act as his proxies and labour in the Afterworld fields instead of him. There were 356 workmen, 36 foremen and 12 overseers, the numbers corresponding to the divisions of the ancient Egyptian year. Some were inscribed with the shabti formula, declaring their function, while others simply bore the name of the king. Most were found in the Annexe, but over 150 others were in the

Left: Tutankhamun's shabti figures, which would be animated in the Afterlife and deputise for the king, are very variable. Some, such as these, are of high quality. They had all originally been kept in wooden caskets and some appear to be portraits of the king, especially the left-hand one. This was a gift to the tomb from Nakhtmin, one of the generals in Tutankhamun's army.

Treasury and a solitary stray was in the Antechamber. They were made in various materials and some are exquisite while others are more mundane; some had been dedicated by two of the king's officials, Nakhtmin and Maya. Associated with them were their implements: 1866 miniature agricultural tools.

One of the figures found may have been more secular in its purpose, though that is only a probability; it is baffling. Howard Carter thought it was a mannequin, a model for either clothing or jewellery, and it may be. The king is shown wearing a yellow headdress but the arms of the figure are cut off below the shoulders, and the body just below the waist; the ears are pierced. The torso is white, the flesh is a reddish-brown – a colour traditionally used to depict male flesh – and the eyebrows, outlines of the eyes and irises are black. The eyes are white, with hints of red at the corners. It remains a mysterious piece.

Above: A sculpture of the head of Tutankhamun emerging from a lotus flower, symbolising the king's rebirth.

Left: This figure, showing Tutankhamun in the act of throwing a spear, is actually an allegory of order defeating chaos. The king represents the god Horus battling the hippopotamus – the god Seth.

Jewellery

The king's mummy had been equipped with 150 items of ritual jewellery, but other pieces were also discovered in the tomb. Originally there had been many more; going by the ancient notes which detailed the contents of boxes, about 60 per cent had been stolen. Most items were found in the Treasury, but odd pieces were found throughout; a few came from the entrance corridor. Parts of a collar, or maybe of two, were even found caught on the rough edges of the resealed hole through the door into the Burial Chamber.

Tutankhamun had been provided with a huge range of jewellery – from finger rings to large collars – and some earrings were found, which he would not have worn after puberty. There are bracelets, amulets, pectoral ornaments and scarabs. Some pieces are elaborate, made from precious materials, while others are basic. Many incorporate a lot of gold, sometimes mixed with other materials to alter the colour, but silver and bronze are also present. Semi-precious stones include carnelian for its red colour, lapis lazuli for blue, amethyst, turquoise, and serpentine; faience and glass occur in many pieces as well. Many different techniques were evidently used by the royal jewellers, too, and the skills represented in the jewellery cannot be over-emphasised. Stringing a complicated collar or strapped pectoral necklace was detailed and painstaking work, just as much as manufacturing the individual elements. Special titles were given to royal jewellers and goldsmiths, and they seem to have enjoyed a high social position.

Jewellery workshops were specialised places, some concentrating on making beads and stringing them, some on assembling necklaces and larger pieces but not on manufacturing the individual elements, which were made elsewhere. They appear in tomb paintings, and it is possible to see the way in which elaborate pieces were created. In the New Kingdom, beads are shown embedded in either plaster or depressions on the workbench, while a craftsman drills holes in them using a bow drill – one bow operating several drills. Beads were then polished, and they seem to have been almost mass produced. Assembling collars was much more specialised. A similar kind of organisation seems to have been followed in all workshops, with master craftsmen at the top, followed by assistants and apprentices, accompanied by controllers and overseers. Sons tended to follow their fathers, where possible, and those artisans who worked in the royal workshops were the best. Many of them had special titles.

The raw materials they used came from all over the Egyptian empire, some coming as the result of trade – copper, for example, was traded with Cyprus but also originated from western Sinai – and some essentially as tribute. In the earliest times only the king could wear gold, but this privilege was later extended to others, especially priests and highly favoured nobles and courtiers; gold symbolised immortality and was also extremely valuable. Army officers – and other ranks – could receive golden awards for bravery on the field of battle. Metalworkers generally used gold itself over other materials, or as part of an alloy, and cast objects were reserved for gods or kings. Silver had to be imported and iron was both rare and precious, and usually came in the form of finished artefacts from abroad.

Above: Plainer jewellery was also found. This collar, found on the mummy, represents the cobra goddess Wadjet shown with the wings of a falcon or vulture. It would have been included to function as an amulet.

Left: This huge pectoral ornament, nearly 15 cm tall, is an exceptional piece of goldworking. The body of the scarab is translucent green chalcedony, and the whole thing is entirely symbolic.

Opposite: A flexible gold collar representing the vulture goddess Nekhbet had been placed on the king's mummy, covering the chest and extending to the shoulders. The wings are made from 250 segments strung together through eyelets on the reverse. The counterweight – the smaller piece – was designed to hang down the back and balance the whole.

Royal regalia

The tomb did contain items of regalia including crooks and flails, and a sceptre was found in the Annexe. Many pieces were found on the mummy itself, including a diadem of gold and inlay, but there was a marked absence of other items, notably royal headgear. Objects such as this could have been stolen by the thieves but they would have been difficult to dispose of, and it is probably more likely that such things were taken over by Ay, Tutankhamun's successor. A flexible gold corselet was found, which probably classes as regalia; it is certainly impressive and impractical. This had been targeted by the robbers. Most of it was found in a box in the Antechamber, but parts were discovered elsewhere – in the corridor fill, in other boxes and in the small gold shrine. It has a broad collar with a pectoral plaque showing Tutankhamun and three gods, and the main part, which would have gone round the body and been secured by slide fasteners, has shoulder straps. It is made from gold, richly inlaid, and is still incomplete – the thieves evidently managed to get away with some of it.

Below: An enamelled pectoral in the form of a vulture, representing the goddess Nekhbet. It had been placed around the neck of the dead king.

Above: This three-scarab pectoral necklace was found in the mummy wrappings. The discs above the outer scarabs are made of a gold and copper alloy and represent the sun; the central one is a mixture of gold and silver and represents the moon.

Opposite above: This exceptionally heavy scarab bracelet was discovered in a box found in the Treasury. It is clearly symbolic but it does show signs of wear and was made for someone with small, thin arms – the young king, presumably. It is formed of two semi-circles joined by a hinge and a clasp, allowing the rigid bracelet to be opened and worn comfortably.

Opposite: This inlaid pectoral depicts the scarab beetle Khepri, the newborn sun god. The scene spells out the throne name of Tutankhamun: Nebkheperure, meaning 'Re is the Lord of Manifestations.'

Remodelled jewels

A significant amount of the jewellery found in Tutankhamun's tomb seems to have been recycled, like many other objects it contained. Some things, like a bracelet with Akhenaten's name, still bear the cartouches of the earlier owner; on others the names have been changed. Sometimes the alterations are marked by a difference in technique and sometimes the hieroglyphics of the name are incorrectly oriented or set inelegantly, perhaps in a cartouche designed for a longer royal name, making the change obvious.

The jewellery was not simply beautiful and rich. It was also symbolic, and hieroglyphics are a regular feature, with elements substituted to change and emphasise meaning, or illustrate the king's names and titles more effectively. The purpose of much of it was to help guarantee the king eternal life.

'Countless others...'

When Howard Carter summed up his first impressions of the Antechamber, he selected some major objects – the couches, the guardian figures – but was careful to stress that there were many other beautiful and fascinating objects: 'countless others'. After all, the king had been provided with everything he would need in the next world.

Tutankhamun would need to be fed in the Afterlife, as would anyone, and an assortment of food and flavourings were provided in his tomb; there was also wine. Foodstuffs were scattered throughout the tomb chambers, but most of them appear to have been originally stored in the Annexe; they appeared to have been one of the groups of things moved by the robbers.

There were pots and baskets which contained both raw grain and loaves of bread; chickpeas and lentils were also found. To flavour and spice his food, Tutankhamun had been provided with garlic, juniper berries – of which he had four whole baskets – fenugreek, sesame, cumin and coriander. There were two jars of honey, which was used for sweetening wine and beer as well as food. There were dates, palm fruits, dried grapes and other types of fruit. Dates seem to have been universally popular in Ancient Egypt, and were used as a sweetener by those who could not afford the rather more luxurious honey; they were also valued for their medicinal virtues (amongst other things they were believed to aid fertility). Palm fruits were either eaten raw, soaked in water or made into syrup. Tutankhamun had also been left almonds and watermelon seeds, though the latter might have been intended for planting rather than eating.

Some of the first things seen by Carter and Carnarvon as they entered the Antechamber were a number of white-painted, curved wooden boxes stowed beneath the legs of one of the three large couches, the middle one which was almost opposite the entrance. These boxes proved to be coated with black resin on the inside, and contained joints of meat. The specific cut each was supposed to contain was docketed on the outside, but this rarely matched whatever the box actually had in it – another example of the confusion often apparent around Tutankhamun's burial. But this substitution was not completely random, there was some order: those boxes which should have contained ox heads, for example, had shoulder joints instead. It has been suggested that the boxes were marked up in advance but that the appropriate joints had not been sent, so the people filling the containers still grouped what they had got, even though the precise descriptions no longer matched.

Opposite: The scenes of an ostrich hunt on this golden fan from the Burial Chamber reflect the inscription, which records that the feathers were from ostriches killed by the king while hunting. There were originally 42 feathers, alternately brown and white, but only their stumps remain. The rest have been eaten by insects.

Left: A wooden model of a falcon, covered in gold leaf and inlaid. The precise meaning of many items in the tomb can only be guessed at, but their beauty and the skill of their makers is immediately apparent.

Below: The board game senet was extremely popular, so much so that it developed a ritual significance and became an allegory of the final judgement. Unfortunately not much is known about the rules or how the game was played, though there have been many suggestions.

There were many items with a clear religious significance quite apart from the human figures. Gods appear in their animal forms, like the statue of Anubis found in the Treasury; the gilded head of a cow was also found there, for example, a representation of the goddess Hathor, and there were others. There are also an array of things which can only be described as magical objects, like the wooden oars which lay between the outer shrine and the north wall of the Burial Chamber. They may have been connected to the journey the king would make to reach the Afterworld, but that is only a possibility. A few musical instruments were found – two trumpets, a pair of clappers and a pair of sistra, ritual rattles. There are so few that they were probably also included for their ritual significance.

A lot of writing material – ink palettes, pigments used for making ink, a pen case and other items – had been buried with Tutankhamun. Some of the items seemed to have been used while others were heavy funerary objects which would have been impractical. These may have been important because the king was believed to become scribe to the sun god after his death, according to the comprehensive Old Kingdom Pyramid Texts. No significant documents on papyrus were found with Tutankhamun – they may have been removed by the tomb robbers – though there were many inscriptions and notes in both formal hieroglyphics and the more rapid and practical form of writing known as hieratic.

Left: This fan, covered in gold foil, was found in the Burial Chamber. Like many items in the tomb, it bears the king's name. Like all Egyptian rulers Tutankhamun had five. Tutankhamun, originally Tutankaten, was his personal name held from birth and adapted to reflect the return to the old religion. His throne name was Nebkheperure and the two names Nebkheperure and Tutankhamun, often appear together in cartouches (the oval shapes) as they do here.

Opposite: A detail of the painted box. Each of the long sides is decorated with a painting of Tutankhamun riding his chariot, defeating the enemies of Egypt. On the lid he is shown hunting wild animals including lions, antelope and ostriches.

Right: This cosmetic jar, almost 29 cm tall, is one of the many stone vessels found. Most, like this one which was found in the Burial Chamber, were made of calcite and most had been emptied - probably during the second of the two robberies. When the tomb was tidied up afterwards, some of the now empty jars were used to contain small things which had been thrown around the tomb by the thieves.

Other items clearly had a secular role, as well as a religious one. The ancient Egyptians seem to have been very fond of board games and Tutankhamun had four complete game boards, all of which were found in the Annexe. One universally popular game was senet – the name means 'passing' – which was played on a board of 30 squares divided equally into three rows. It developed from a game which was simply included in a tomb in order to provide amusement in the Afterlife into an element of religious ritual and is often depicted in tomb paintings; the immortality of the deceased was at stake.

The famous painted box is but one of many boxes and chests. One of the others shows the king and queen together. It is composed of a series of ivory panels, with a larger carved and painted one set into each side, and into the lid. At the end is a scene of Tutankhamun and Ankhesenamun sitting in a lush landscape by a rectangular pool full of fish; he is shooting at wildfowl with a bow and arrow while she sits at his feet. An attendant is approaching, carrying a duck and a fish, both

killed by the king. The rest of the panel is entirely filled with floral decoration. The lid shows the queen giving flowers to the king.

The guardian statues from the Antechamber had long staffs, and many such ceremonial staffs and walking sticks were found in the tomb; some showed signs of having been used. There were also eight fans, a sign of status. One was designed to be held in the hand and was found in a box; its feathers survived, something not true of the others. One of the most beautiful was found between the third and fourth shrines in the Burial Chamber. It is covered in thick gold foil and both sides are embossed and chased; on one the king is shown hunting ostrich and on the other he returns from the hunt in triumph. Inscriptions say that the ostrich feathers – now mostly long gone – were obtained by the king 'hunting in the desert east of Heliopolis'. This, like everything else from the tomb, is a remarkable voice from the past, a window into the world of well over 3000 years ago.

The Curse of Tutankhamun

On 28 February 1923, Lord Carnarvon left the Valley of the Kings and travelled to Aswan for a few days' break. He was bitten by a mosquito on the cheek either shortly after he arrived or during the journey, and he accidentally opened the bite while he was shaving. Though he attempted to treat it with iodine, infection set in and he developed a fever. He allowed his daughter Evelyn to confine him to bed; after two days he felt much better, got up and expressed a desire to return to the excavation – and suffered a relapse. He was moved to Cairo where he could receive better medical care but pneumonia developed and he died during the early hours of 5 April. He was 57.

Legends immediately began to spread. Carnarvon's death, it was suggested, had been caused by 'ominous forces', by the revenge of the disturbed pharaoh. His dog, still at home in England, was supposed to have howled and then died inexplicably at the very hour of its owner's death; all the lights in

Cairo had gone out at just that moment… Actually, there was no mystery. Carnarvon's health was fragile and had been so for many years, ever since the car accident which had led him to spend the winters in Egypt, and the infected mosquito bite had simply led to blood poisoning. Cairo's electrical system at the time was somewhat unreliable, so the lights may well have gone off; it cannot be confirmed whether they did or not. There is no independent verification of the story of the dog, either.

A supposed inscription – 'Death will come on swift wings to he who breaches the tomb of pharaoh' – is another myth. An inscription was found on a brick lying in front of the Anubis shrine in the Treasury, but it said 'I am the one preventing the sand from blocking the chamber'. Curses have been found in some Egyptian tombs, warnings not to damage the tomb coupled with threats of dire consequences. These are, however, mostly in private tombs, and are generally Old Kingdom in date. There is actually a marked absence of curses from royal tombs and where they are included they are mostly concerned with speaking ill of the dead rather than damaging or entering the tomb.

Soon other alleged omens were connected to the tomb as well, and the story of the curse was firmly entrenched. Anyone who died and who could be associated with the excavation, however remotely, had their demise linked to the 'curse'. But once again reality is rather more down-to-earth. Of the 22 people who had been present when the sarcophagus was opened, most were still alive 10 years later; only 6 had died. Carnarvon's daughter Evelyn had been one of the first people into the tomb; she died in 1980 at the age of 79. Howard Carter was 64 when he died in 1939; Harry Burton, the expedition's photographer, died in 1940 at the age of 60. Alan Gardiner, who had worked on the inscriptions, was 84 when he died in 1963; Douglas Derry, the doctor who autopsied the king's mummy – surely a prime candidate for any effective vengeful curse – died in 1969 aged 87. But the curse was a good story, and good stories never seem to go away in the face of actual evidence. Certainly if there was any truth in the curse of Tutankhamun, and there is none whatsoever, then it took a remarkably long time to catch up with most of the main people involved. With everyone except Lord Carnarvon, in fact.

Opposite: Despite persistent rumours to the contrary, most members of the team connected to the opening and exploration of Tutankhamun's tomb lived for many years after its discovery. The doctor who autopsied the pharaoh's body, for example, was 87 when he died in 1969. Here are some key members of the excavation team in 1923, from left to right: Arthur Mace, Reginald Engelbach, Howard Carter, Alfred Lucas, Arthur Callender and Harry Burton.

Above: Lord Carnarvon was the only person closely connected with Tutankhamun's tomb who died soon after the discovery. His death was a result of blood poisoning following a mosquito bite which became infected.

Left: This unusual wooden statue of the king may have been a mannequin used for fitting the king's clothing and jewellery (the ears are pierced), but this is just a possibility. It remains a mysterious object.

INDEX

BIBLIOGRAPHY

Baines, J. and Malek, J., Cultural Atlas of Ancient Egypt, New York, 2000 edn

Carter, H. and Mace, A.C., The Tomb of Tut.ankh.amun, London 1923–33 (3 vols)

David, R. and Achbold, R., Conversations with Mummies: New Light on the Ancient Egyptians, London, 2000

Davies, V. and Friedman, R., Egypt, London, 1998

Desroches-Noblecourt, C., Life and Death of a Pharoah: Tutankhamun, London, 1963

Edwards, I E S., The Treasures of Tutakhamun (exhibition catalogue), London, 1972

Kemp, B.J., Ancient Egypt: Anatomy of a Civilization, London, 1989

Reeves, N., The Complete Tutankhamun, London, 1990 (new edition, 2007)

Reeves, N. and Wilkinson, R.H., The Complete Valley of the Kings, London, 1996

Shaw, I., (ed) Oxford History of Ancient Egypt, Oxford, 2000

Strouhal, E., Life in Ancient Egypt, Cambridge, 1992

Strudwick, N. and Strudwick, H., Thebes in Egypt, London, 1999

Taylor, J., Death and the Afterlife in Ancient Egypt, London, 2001

Tiradritti, F. (ed), Treasures of the Egyptian Museum, Cairo, 1999

Watterson, B., Amarna: Egypt's Age of Revolution, Stroud, 1999

Acknowledgements

The publisher would like to thank the following photographers and picture libraries for their kind permission to reproduce their image in this book:

Art and Architecture Collection Ltd

44, 47(r), 69, 82, 86(t), 87(t); R. Sheridan/Art and Architecture Collection Ltd 2, 14(b), 16, 23, 24, 25(t&b), 27, 28, 29(t&b), 34, 38(t), 39, 48, 55(l), 61, 63, 72, 74, 75(b), 77 (r&l), 78, 79(b), 81(t&b), 83(l), 85(t&b), 89(b); Danita Delemont/Art and Architecture Collection Ltd 10; M. Jelliffe/Art and Architecture Collection Ltd 8–9, 14(t), 45, 62(t&b), 75(t); R. Ashworth/Art and Architecture Collection Ltd 17(b); C.M. Dixon/Art and Architecture Collection Ltd 36, 40, 79(t); John P. Stevens/Art and Architecture Collection Ltd 11, 32, 33, 38(b); Dr. S. Coyne/Art and Architecture Collection Ltd 41; Prisma/Art and Architecture Collection Ltd 42; R. Bell/Art and Architecture Collection Ltd 49; B. Norman/Art and Architecture Collection Ltd 60

Corbis:
3, 4–5, 6, 12–13, 15, 19(t), 20(b),26 (t&b), 30–31, 35(l&r), 37, 43 (l&r), 46, 47(l), 50–51, 52, 55(r), 57(t), 59, 65(b), 66, 68, 71, 73, 76, 80, 83(r), 84, 88, 89(t), 90(t&b), 91, 92, 93(b)

Getty Images:
1, 18, 20(t), 21, 22, 53, 56, 57(b), 64, 65(t), 67, 70, 86(b), 87(b), 93(t)